Praise for *Your Money God's Way*

"Too many believers stumble through life with no plan for their money, asking God to bless their carelessness. That's not how it works! In *Your Money God's Way*, Amie Streater cuts through the "churchy talk" and delivers a powerful message of common sense and biblical wisdom that today's churchgoers desperately need."

— DAVE RAMSEY,
Best-Selling Author of *The Total Money Makeover*
and Host of *The Dave Ramsey Show*

"Amie is passionate about helping people get free from crippling debt and the snares of bad spending decisions. This book is for those who are serious about getting help. Prepare to be challenged, corrected, and most of all, equipped to see your personal financial world from a biblical viewpoint."

— BRADY BOYD,
Senior Pastor, New Life Church
Colorado Springs, CO

"Preaching motivates us and tells us *why* we should do something. Teaching equips us and tells us *how* to do it. Most believers are motivated to get their finances in order and know why they should do it, yet they don't know how. Pastor Amie Streater is one of the best financial teachers in the Body of Christ. *Your Money God's Way* will equip you and truly teach you how to live the blessed life God intended all of His children to live.

— ROBERT MORRIS,
A... *Life*;
y Church,

"As someone who has wa... Amie Streater brings solid biblical knowledge ...yone seeking answers for their personal financi... ...ment. I have seen compassionate pastoral care laced with solid biblical answers in Amie's ministry to people. She brings this same combination through written form in this new book. If you want solid biblical answers with proven practical steps to address your financial confusion, this book is for you."

— TOM LANE,
Executive Senior Pastor, Gateway Church,
Dallas–Fort Worth, TX

Testimonials

"God knew we were in dire straits with our finances when He brought Amie into our lives. She taught us that we were dealing with numbers on a page, and that it was God's calling on our lives that really mattered. We went from being 'credit slaves' to 'children of God.' It was transformational! We learned the steps to financial freedom, and now we know how to be good stewards of God's money. Without Amie we would not know the financial peace we now possess."

— JOSEPH AND MENCHIE LITTLEFIELD
New Life Church, Colorado Springs, CO

"As a single mother, there are always moments of wanting to give up or allowing the enemy in with his many, many distractions. But with Amie by my side, I was able to stay focused and on track for getting my finances in order and getting out of debt. She is always honest but also tough when she needs to be. Through her tough love, I've learned to rely more on God and practice God's ways regarding finances. We are only stewards of what He puts into our hands. Thank you, Amie, for not judging my bad financial habits, and for desiring the best for me and my daughter."

— MARI GARCIA
Gateway Church, Southlake, TX

"We went into our initial meeting with Amie with much fear and trepidation. We had made a mess of things, and we knew it. What would she say? Would she laugh at us? Would she tell us the things most important to us (eating healthy, having two cars, having Mommy home with the kids) were absurd for someone in our financial condition? To our surprise, what she offered us was understanding, kindness, prayer, personal stories, and encouragement. We had a lot of hard work in front of us, but we could see a path to freedom from debt for the first time. We did some crying, but we did a whole lot more laughing. Amie makes getting out of debt fun, somehow! We feel like we have our life back."

— SARA AND NICK MICHALSKI
New Life Church, Colorado Springs, CO

"We are eternally grateful to Amie for being the voice of wise counsel for our family over the last two years. She has patiently and lovingly shared her wisdom and knowledge of biblical financial stewardship, which has forever changed our lives. She has cried with us when our situation looked impossible, rejoiced with us when we saw breakthrough, and we could trust her to always keep us on the path of stewardship. Our family tree has been altered because of her investment into the Sahhar family. After reading the words in this book, yours will be, too!"

— CHAD AND LEAH SAHHAR
New Life Church, Colorado Springs, CO

"My friend Amie Streater has the goods when it comes to good stewardship and faithfulness with what God has given to her. We served together on the pastoral staff at Gateway Church in Southlake, TX. When I needed a financial tip or advice, I stuck my head in Amie's office, and she always led me to the latest and best Web site to answer my questions. Whether it was clipping coupons or checking *Consumer Reports* before purchasing a new car, she was on top of it. I sent a number of people to Amie for financial coaching and advice. I wasn't a bit surprised to hear that Amie had put her vast knowledge and experience in writing to help the multitudes. I love her practical and yet bold approach to good stewardship. You go, girl!"

— LINDA GODSEY
Associate Pastor, Freedom Ministries,
Gateway Church, Southlake, TX

"Amie Streater is a woman with a calling to destroy debt and bring people from shame and discouragement to a place of practical wisdom and hope and biblical financial sense! She was an answer to prayer for my wife, Tracy, and me. We knew we needed help. We just needed someone to walk with us through the muck and the mire. She not only did that, but she never once shamed us in the process for what we should have, could have, and wish we would have done! She was Jesus with skin on to us, and we will always be forever grateful. We aren't out of the woods yet, but we're finally on the right path!"

— DANIEL AND TRACY AMSTUTZ
New Life Church, Colorado Springs, CO

"It wasn't long into my lunch with Amie that I burst into tears and interrupted what she was saying to tell her that my house was in foreclosure. Finally, I had found a safe place to share my burden. As someone who has held leadership positions in the church, and as a professional, I was consumed by shame that I was in this position. Through Amie's ministry I discovered I'm not the only one in the church who was carrying a secret financial burden. By sharing my burden and allowing others to teach and love on me, I have found freedom."

— CATHERINE HAMMOND
New Life Church, Colorado Springs, CO

"Amie's story will rock your world. She is honest, caring, and speaks the truth in love. She wants you to succeed, and she knows that by surrounding herself with many wise counselors, she will be successful. Let her be to you wise counsel in this book so that you are successful in all that God has called you to do. She has become a little sister to me—one that I will love and cherish for a lifetime."

— CAROL TRELSTAD
New Life Church, Colorado Springs, CO

"Amie is the red-haired angel whom God sent to give us hope! The many times we doubted God was listening to our prayers for our financial situation, Amie would kick us in the backside and show us through Scripture, conversation, and sometimes cajoling that we would be okay. Her ability to make us stronger allowed us to help others walking down the same path, and this helped us heal and gather hope. Hope is what Amie gave to us, and through her writing she will give you this same hope, along with God's love, provision, understanding, and knowing when we foul things up, He is still there and He still loves us. Thank you so very much, Amie, we love you dearly."

— BRENT AND LINDA EBAUGH
New Life Church, Colorado Springs, CO

YOUR
MONEY
GOD'S WAY

YOUR MONEY GOD'S WAY

OVERCOMING THE 7 MONEY MYTHS THAT KEEP CHRISTIANS BROKE

AMIE STREATER

THOMAS NELSON
Since 1798

NASHVILLE   DALLAS   MEXICO CITY   RIO DE JANEIRO

Published in Nashville, Tennessee, by Thomas Nelson. Thomas Nelson is a registered trademark of Thomas Nelson, Inc.

Thomas Nelson, Inc., titles may be purchased in bulk for educational, business, fund-raising, or sales promotional use. For information, please e-mail SpecialMarkets@ThomasNelson.com.

Unless otherwise marked, all Scripture quotations are taken from the NEW KING JAMES VERSION. © 1982 by Thomas Nelson, Inc. Used by permission. All rights reserved.

This book is intended to provide accurate information with regard to the subject matter covered. However, the Author and the Publisher accept no responsibility for inaccuracies or omissions, and the Author and Publisher specifically disclaim any liability, loss, or risk, whether personal, financial, or otherwise, that is incurred as a consequence, directly or indirectly, from the use and/or application of any of the contents of this book.

This book is based, in part, on true events, but certain liberties have been taken with names, places, and dates, and the characters have been invented. Therefore, the persons and characters portrayed bear absolutely no resemblance whatever to the persons who were actually involved in the events described in this book.

Library of Congress Cataloging-in-Publication Data

Streater, Amie.
    Your money God's way : overcoming the 7 money myths that keep Christians broke / Amie Streater.
        p. cm.
    ISBN 978-1-59555-232-7
    1. Wealth—Religious aspects—Christianity. 2. Money—Religious aspects—Christianity. I. Title.
BR115.W4S76 2010
241'.68—dc22   2010012218

Printed in the United States of America

11 12 13 14 RRD 5

To my darling husband, Scott, whose patience, kindness, love, and laughter make every day a joy. There are no words for how much I love you. You are God's greatest blessing to me.

In memory of my grandmother, Wanda Holland. I cannot imagine that God ever created a woman of stronger faith, greater resilience, and deeper love. Thank you, Nana, for all you poured into me. I miss you every day.

And for all the families at New Life Church in Colorado Springs, Colorado, and Gateway Church in Southlake, Texas, who have shared their lives with me and trusted me for guidance during their darkest hours and times of tested faith. Thank you for the honor of allowing me to serve and pastor you.

CONTENTS

PREFACE

Let me tell you about my moment.

I was cruising down the freeway in Fort Worth one beautiful spring day, on my way home from my wonderful job as a not-so-mild-mannered reporter for a major metropolitan newspaper. I was in one of my designer suits, Ferragamos on my pedicured feet, my manicured hands on the steering wheel of my fabulous fifty-thousand-dollar leased SUV, while my hair—with a fresh, seventy-five-dollar haircut—shimmered in the Texas sunlight streaming in from the sunroof. I was privileged enough to be driving to a beautiful house in one of the most coveted suburbs in the area, where, after greeting our children's nanny in the housekeeper-scrubbed foyer, I would prepare a fabulous dinner, then take a dip in the pool or perhaps soak in the waterfall hot tub.

My husband and I made good money. Our infant twins and pre-school son were healthy and happy. We were mighty blessed.

And we were flat broke.

The beautiful home was mortgaged to the hilt. We were fourteen thousand dollars upside down on the "fabulous" leased SUV. My clothes, the kids' clothes, the haircuts, the makeup, the shoes—all of it went on credit cards. The bills were piling up, but I figured the debt was just part of living my "fabulous" life.

But something inside of me was becoming deeply and profoundly uncomfortable. After making all the minimum credit card payments, sometimes I didn't have enough money left over to pay for groceries. So I put the groceries on a credit card, along with the diapers and the gasoline.

There was an emotional shift at home as well: Scott and I started to get really agitated whenever something broke around the house because we knew we didn't have the money to fix it. We were tense and unhappy, in spite of our house full of stuff.

While I had not yet realized just how bad things had actually gotten, I knew deep down that we were headed to a bad place financially and that the slightest unexpected financial setback could send our life crashing down around us.

Fortunately, on that fateful spring day, something happened before I made it home, something that would change my life forever.

Our children's nanny, Melissa, had become a trusted friend, and I had let her in on our little secret that things were not as perfect as they looked. In response, Melissa bought me some CDs of sermons taught at her church—about money. I put the CDs in the car to listen to on the commute to work, but I was skeptical. *What is some pastor going to tell me about money? I know all about money!* I thought. But I listened. And on the way home that day, I heard a sermon called "The 90-Day Challenge," taught by some guy I had never heard of before, named Jeff Drott.

As I listened to him tell his honest and heartbreaking story of losing everything yet finding God, and then learning how to manage what God had entrusted to him, God reached a place in my heart that had been untouched for a very long time. I had been in church thousands of Sundays but never knew God cared how we manage our money.

He does.

In the sermon, Pastor Jeff used a funny, churchy-sounding word that I had never heard before—*stewardship*—and it pierced my heart like a dagger. My mind was spinning in a way that even now is hard for me to explain. It was like taking a final exam and realizing that half the test was based on a chapter I had accidentally skipped over. I felt panicked. *Stewardship? What? What is that? Why do I not know about stewardship? How did I not know that the Bible teaches about money management?* Suddenly I realized that everything I thought I knew about money and how to manage it was not only wrong, it was in direct violation of what the Bible teaches about finances. And even after all those Sunday school lessons and church sermons, I had absolutely no idea how polluted my head, heart, emotions, and attitudes had become.

That's when I felt the gentle whisper of the Holy Spirit speaking directly to my materialistic little heart: *Honey, you missed this.*

If you miss this lesson called stewardship, you miss *everything.*

When you spend more than you earn, your whole life is a lie. *My* whole life was a lie. A charade. A house of fancy cards that was ready to topple over. I began to cry so hard that I had to pull over on the side of the freeway. I sat there for probably ten minutes or so, just praying and crying out to God to forgive me. To help me fix things. To help me change. What a mess I had created! We had tons of debt and no savings and were highly leveraged on everything from the shoes on my feet right on up to the home that sheltered my family. *How did I let this happen?* I wondered. *How could I be so stupid? How did I miss this?*

I went home and added it all up, all the debt. All the credit cards. All the monthly expenses. The debt was bad—about sixty thousand dollars' worth, just on the credit cards, not even counting the house or the stupid SUV. And because these were the days when "universal default" was still in play, once we made a late payment on one card, the interest on almost all of them went to more than 30 percent. In a matter of months, sixty thousand grew to more than one hundred thousand, even after we started budgeting and trying to do things the "right" way. We had a huge hole to dig out of.

It was not quick; neither was it particularly enjoyable, but eventually, we saw sunlight again. We were very blessed during the process because our house of cards never fell. And we never filed bankruptcy, never lost a house in foreclosure, and never paid a bill more than a little bit late.

But it was hard. We sacrificed. We sold the SUV, happily, and the house, after many tears. We didn't see the inside of a restaurant or a movie theater for a long, long time. And yet, in spite of our sacrifices, trivial as they were compared to the trials of so many, we gained a thousand times more than we gave up: new friends, a whole new way of living, and, finally, peace.

Thank you, God, for that peace.

Your Money God's Way is not about my story, but I wanted to tell you about my "moment" for two reasons: First, this book is bold. I will say things to you that other people don't have the courage to say—or that you may not have the courage to say to yourself. I don't mince words or beat around the bush, and I am not going to baby you. If you're old enough to read this, you're big enough to receive the very kick in the pants you probably need in order to do better with your money. Yet as you read, never think for one second that these words are coming from someone who is looking down her nose at you. Not me.

If you are in a bad place financially, please know that I have been there too. I have cried the tears. I have stayed awake at night, wondering if I should pay the credit cards or the mortgage. I have gotten physically sick more times than I care to admit during bill-paying time. Yes, I've been there.

But one critical moment turned into a life-changing journey for me. So the second and most important reason I've shared my moment with you is that I am hoping you will have a moment of your own. I hope that as you read this book, you will allow God to speak to you and to heal your heart. What's more, I hope you will ask Him to reveal His truth to you. It is only through God's truth that we can ever be free.

We got a lot of bad advice from well-meaning people during the early days of trying to clean up our mess. Fortunately, as we fumbled around for some truth, we found two things that genuinely helped us: Christian financial coaches and Dave Ramsey's Financial Peace University.

Once things started improving for us, we were so excited about what we had learned that we began volunteering at our church (yes, we joined the church that produced the CDs our nanny had given us), Gateway Church in Southlake, Texas. We began in faith to help others with their financial problems, even as we continued to work through our struggles with our own. And during that time, I hounded the pastors so often with ideas on financial stewardship that they eventually asked me to come on staff, probably so I would just shut up and implement the plans myself. So I did. I left my journalism career and went into ministry, becoming a pastor who specializes in biblical financial education.

A couple of years later, I got to meet that guy, Jeff Drott, who'd had the nerve to preach a sermon on money and get into my business that day on the Fort Worth freeway. He hired me for my current position at New Life Church in Colorado Springs. What a joy it was to tell him that before he had ever met me, his story had changed my life.

God *always* has a plan.

Because I have worked at two very large churches, I've had the opportunity to meet thousands of people in varying degrees of financial health. Unfortunately, many of them are in economic crisis. It breaks my heart to see good Christian families go through the heartbreak of foreclosure, the agony of debt, and the misery of divorce brought on by money problems. The good news is, though occasionally financial upheaval cannot be avoided, 99 percent of the time it can. In the following chapters, there is truth that will help any family either recover from or avoid a fiscal catastrophe.

If you are doing great with your money, congratulations. This book will help you stay on the financial mountaintop and avoid the pitfalls that ensnare most everyone else. Read carefully with an open and humble heart and remember: "There, but for the grace of God, go I." If you're struggling with your money, take heart. God has a plan for you. He has a purpose and a calling for your life that is unique to you, and He can take you there, even from where you are right now.

One of the most fascinating things I've seen in my ministry is that while many families can be experiencing the same general type of financial distress, such as unmanageable credit card debt, foreclosure, etc., the root causes are different for every family, and each needs a particular solution. The way God uses individualized ways to walk different families out of financial distress is nothing short of miraculous. It's as if He has a personal financial prescription for every family willing to ask Him for it and work hard to achieve it. In *Your Money God's Way*, I will help you figure out what God's prescription is for *your* family.

Once you discover your own path, you will have your own story too. And while I cannot tell you what the twists and turns will be, I can promise you that your story will be different from anyone else's because God designed you, your life, and your calling to be unique.

But in order for God to bless you and change your circumstances, you have to be willing to change *yourself*, or more specifically, your heart, your head, and your convictions. Because if your money is messed up, the problem really *isn't* your money; it's you. That may sound harsh, but it's the truth. Here's why: in Matthew 6:25–31, Jesus promised that our heavenly Father will meet all of our needs. Sure, hard times will come, and bad things will occasionally happen to good people, but if you are in a systematic pattern of not having enough, it is not because God is not providing for you; it is because you are not managing what He has already given you.

And you know what? Most of us have failed in this area. Some of us, including me, have failed spectacularly, time and time again. The important thing is to recognize when we have weaknesses in this area, figure out what those weaknesses are, and then take steps to overcome them. That is what this book is about.

Your Money God's Way isn't a "how to get out of debt" book, a savings book, or a budgeting book. It is a book about why you're not doing those things already, and as you read, you will finally begin to understand *why* you don't do the things you say you want to do with your money. More important, you will learn simple steps and timeless truths to help you change those habits—for good. Understanding brings change. And understanding *why* you make the decisions you make regarding your money is the first step to making better decisions.

Imagine what your life would be like if you never again had to worry about money. Envision how it would feel if you were giving, saving, living below your means—*and* having fun with your money. Now picture going to sleep and knowing that all the bills are paid, your nest egg is being funded, you have cash set aside for a rainy day, and through your generosity, others less fortunate than you are being helped. Wouldn't that feel good? Wouldn't you like to have that feeling?

You *can*, and you can have it much sooner than you think. But you'll have to work hard to challenge your beliefs and start thinking about money as God does.

God's way is always better than our way. Understanding how to manage your money God's way is the key to ending your economic worries forever and living the financial life God designed for you.

INTRODUCTION

"Why, God?"

"Why did God let this happen to us?"

Day after day, people file into my office with one financial catastrophe after another. After they run down the difficulties of the past months and years, the first question they ask is usually, "Why did God let this happen to us?" And because I have the title of "Pastor" in front of my name, they are expecting a profound answer, one invoking promising Scriptures (just the peppy ones, please), a dramatic retelling of some biblical miracle, and for bonus points, a cuddly parable or two. They want to cry. They want to whine. They want reassurance that they have been the victims of some insurmountable circumstance that led them to this point. And they want nothing short of an event of biblical proportions to deliver them out of it.

That's what they want. Here's what they get:

"You've done some really dumb things with your money. Really, really, *really* dumb. We're going to spend some time figuring out why you've been doing dumb stuff, and I will show you how to start doing smart stuff. You can fix this, but it won't be easy, and it won't happen overnight. Are you ready?"

The response is typically stunned silence. After all, who goes to a pastor for a challenge? The plain truth is that most of the people coming into my office don't need hugs and tears. They need a swift kick in the rear.

I will venture to guess that you could benefit from the same.

Let me introduce myself. To my students and my church family, I am Pastor Amie, a confidante, coach, cheerleader, teacher, and drill sergeant. My job title is "financial stewardship pastor," which is a churchy way of saying that I am a personal finance coach who happens to know the Bible really well. Most people come through my door or into one of my classes with crippling debt, no savings, bad habits, and a broken heart. Some of them have lost jobs or suffered the death or prolonged illness of a spouse. Some are single parents, suddenly abandoned and left to pay the bills alone. Most of them, however, have been just plain stupid with their money, and now they think it is all God's fault.

I push my people hard. I challenge them. I pray for them, and when needed, I give them that proverbial kick in the pants. I don't sound like most other pastors out there, and that's okay with me because for too long pastors have ignored one of the most common problems plaguing Christian families: financial ignorance. I grew up in the church yet still had to go broke and learn for myself, the hard way, that it's not God's will for us to have a zero balance in the bank, or worse, to be in the red. It's time to put a stop to the ignorance and the silence. It's time for Christian families to stand up, grow up, and seize the inheritance that is theirs. I am committed to helping them do that.

> For too long pastors have ignored one of the most common problems plaguing Christian families: financial ignorance.

This isn't some pie-in-the-sky prosperity theology espousing the notion that God wants you to be rich. He very well may *not* want you to be rich, and furthermore, the Bible warns us many, many times against striving for riches simply for the sake of our own selfish gain.

Proverbs 28:20 says, "A faithful man will abound with blessings, but he who hastens to be rich will not go unpunished."

However, the Bible clearly shows us that there is wisdom and blessing in being debt free and having money saved for the future. You don't have to be rich, but you *certainly* don't have to be broke. And consider for a moment that generosity is a prevailing theme of Scripture. How are you going to be generous if you're broke?

You can be generous with your time, of course, and you can be generous of spirit, but your time and good nature are of little use to a starving child in Africa or a missionary who is trying to build water wells in Central America, unless you are personally there, serving those impoverished nations yourself.

Jesus didn't die on the cross so you could lie awake at night, wondering how you're going to make the mortgage payment. That is not the "Victory in Jesus" we sing about in church. In most cases, our financial stresses are self-imposed. And we have to break free from our bad habits if we want to walk in freedom.

I can talk the talk because I walk the walk. I used to be one of those broke believers, crying out to God and asking, "Why?" We had the crippling debt, the empty savings account, the house we couldn't afford, and the overpriced vehicle in the driveway. I've had designer shoes on my feet—and an empty heart. I've had the pool boy come service the hot tub, while wondering how I would pay the house payment. I've lived in posh poverty. And that was when things still looked pretty good on the outside. When all illusions of "posh" went away, I bought my family's food on credit, not out of convenience, but because I didn't have the money in the bank to pay with cash or debit card. And as I stood there, I prayed silently that the card wouldn't be declined.

I've juggled utility bills because I didn't have money to cover them all after I made the minimum payments on my credit cards. I've raided piggy banks to buy school lunches, and I've sold useful things on Craigslist simply because I needed the money. I've run to the mailbox out of desperation, hoping that a check would come when we really,

really needed it. I've not gone to the doctor when I was sick, out of concern for the cost and to make sure the money was available if one of the children got sick.

I've cried into my pillow many nights. I've ducked into my car to "go to the grocery store" so my kids wouldn't see me lose it after paying the bills. I've lost more nights of sleep than I care to recall, wondering *how in the world* we would ever get out of our mess.

I'm done with all of that, and you should be too.

I've coached hundreds of families from all walks of life. In the past three years alone, families under my leadership have paid off more than $6 million in debt. So I know a thing or two about cleaning up messes. And I can say one thing for sure: Christians, as a whole, are worse with money and have a harder time fixing their mistakes than any other group. The reasons why are what this book is all about.

> Christians, as a whole, are worse with money and have a harder time fixing their mistakes than any other group.

Seven key spiritual conditions most often cause Christians to fail in meeting personal financial goals. And regardless of how spiritually mature or financially grounded we think we are, each of us has struggled with at least one of them at one time or another. Most people in financial distress are dealing with some of these right now:

1. Unrealistic, unbiblical beliefs about the power money has to improve our lives
2. A habit of trying to be a savior by continually bailing reckless people out of their messes, and wasting our own resources in the process
3. Polluted theology, which we use to mask laziness and justify not working or failing to work up to our full potential
4. Naïveté about the intentions of others

5. Failure to give, or a tendency to give with the wrong intentions
6. Denial about our current circumstances or the consequences of our actions
7. A tendency to blame God for our own impulsive behavior

It took years of mistakes, prayer, hard work, setbacks, and more prayer to diagnose the real root cause of my own financial failures and, eventually, to help others do the same. But if you will take the lessons in this book to heart and follow the solution steps in each chapter, your own path to financial freedom will be much shorter and involve significantly less pain and fewer setbacks than if you try to fix things on your own.

We're going to be dealing with some deep and difficult heart issues in the chapters to come, and I'm going to really challenge you to dig deep and question whether what you *think* you know about God and money actually lines up with what the Bible tells us about the subject. If you're really digging, you're bound to get uncomfortable. That's okay. Frankly, it's my goal to make you uncomfortable.

My sense of urgency comes not from arrogance or being uncaring, but out of genuine concern for what can happen if you don't get these truths down, if you don't change, if you don't fix your money problems once and for all. My edginess comes from outright anger that any of us tolerate the financial stresses and grief we accept as a normal part of the American life. It's a lie that you have to be in debt in America, and you have to break free from that lie if you're ever going to be truly happy.

It's worse than just being broke: money problems cause divorce; they ruin friendships and family relationships and cause problems with our children. They infect our prayer life and our ability to connect with God.

Whether you make $25,000 a year or $250,000, it doesn't matter. There are wealthy people and poor people at both ends of that spectrum. Actually, there are a lot more poor people. And I don't want you to be one of them.

Your wealth—or lack thereof—is a direct result of the decisions you have made regarding every dollar that has passed through your hands. Owning that truth is a powerful thing, but it's difficult to accept. Most Christians never get there.

You, however, can get there if you will go to that uncomfortable place and listen to what God wants to tell you about your behavior and attitudes toward your money.

Time to Get Free

I started working in ministry after fifteen years as an investigative newspaper reporter. Quite a career change, I know, but I felt called by the words of Isaiah 61:1: "The Spirit of the Lord GOD is upon Me, because the LORD has anointed Me to preach good tidings to the poor; He has sent Me to heal the brokenhearted, to proclaim liberty to the captives and the opening of the prison to those who are bound." Imagine my surprise when I discovered that many of "the poor" didn't want good tidings. They didn't want their prisons opened either. They wanted to wallow in their various misfortunes, to justify their mistakes and spiritualize a financial life marked with neglect and bad decisions, such as maintaining lifestyles they couldn't possibly afford, racking up more and more debt, not giving to their churches, and failing to work "heartily, as to the Lord and not to men," as we are instructed in Colossians 3:23.

If they wanted someone to nod in silence while they gave their laundry list of "reasons" for doing the dumb things they were doing, they came to the wrong pastor. After helping so many families, I've come to understand that it takes more than just teaching the steps to get out of debt—it takes confrontation of the wrong thinking that got them there to begin with.

Even though we may never meet, I'm going to assume a couple of things about you. First, you're probably a lot smarter than your financial habits might indicate. You know in your head what you should do with your money. Live on a budget. Save. Pay off your debt. Set aside 15 percent or more for retirement. Are you doing any of these things? Probably not, and not because you don't know about them but because there are things going on in your heart that keep you from doing what your head knows you need to do to get financially healthy.

> There are things going on in your heart that keep you from doing what your head knows you need to do to get financially healthy.

Second, I'm going to guess that if we can reveal a few simple, biblical truths and get some junk out of your spiritual life, you can start doing the things you've always known you should do.

Money is not complicated. It's not mysterious. It's an inanimate object that we use to get the things we need and want. How we use that tool, however, is a barometer of our spiritual condition because our relationship with money is a reflection of what is going on with our hearts. It's an outward sign of the health of our character. Most Americans have characters so sick they're worthy of a call to 9-1-1, but it takes a healthy and mature person to use money wisely and beneficially. The simple truth is that the rules of money are not hard. And as a bonus, followers of Christ have the promises of God to bless the work of our hands and prosper us.

So, why are so many Christians broke?

Wrong ideas. Wrong thinking. Wrong expectations. And it is easy to get these things wrong when we're suffering from one or more of the above mentioned faulty spiritual conditions. We lose our way, and we neglect to look at the road map God has provided for us, the Bible. While we wouldn't expect to drive a car recklessly without crashing, many Christians think they can run through the mall, waving credit cards consequence-free because "God will provide" when the bill comes.

We can do better than that.

Christians are uniquely gifted at overspiritualizing a practical matter such as personal finance. They cherry-pick Bible verses and use them to justify bad decisions. They do dumb things and pin the fallout on God. And once they have something wrong in their heads, or worse, in their hearts, getting it out takes an act of the very God they're blaming for their problems.

> **Our relationship with money is a reflection of what is going on with our hearts.**

Some of my students joke that my desk is warped from the constant flow of tears in my office. And those tears are warranted, believe me. For the precious few who really have been victims of their circumstances, I cry with them, we pray, and we outline plans to do the best we can with what's before them, asking for God's blessings on their circumstances. That's for the few.

Just about everyone else needs to dry the tears and get busy.

I can't promise you that you will clean up your mess overnight, but I can guarantee that if you follow the principles outlined in this book, you will fix your financial mistakes and they will stay fixed— for the rest of your life. These are simple, biblical truths taught in plain language. God didn't set out to confuse us. It is the bad teaching of pastors with an agenda—to get your donations—that has polluted what Christians *think* they know about what the Bible says about money.

The time has come for truth, simplicity, and freedom, so we can live our lives lined up with the promises of God.

Are you ready?

Let me share with you a prayer that I pray myself quite often. It has gotten me through many a dark day and made the good days a little brighter. You should pray this every day. You can even pray it ten times a day if it helps you because God never gets tired of hearing from you. But whether you use these words or your own, just pray. God is listening.

Dear Jesus, thank You for loving me, for staying beside me, for holding me up when I fall. Please give me an open mind and an open heart. Let me see things as You see them. Show me what's truth. Show me where I am wrong. Open the doors You want me to walk through, and close the ones that lead to places You don't want me to be.

Please bless my efforts to improve my finances. Multiply my resources, and bless me so I may be a blessing to others. Most important, line up my thoughts with Your thoughts. Help me forgive myself for the mistakes of my past, and forgive others for mistakes against me, just as You forgive me for all my sins as soon as I ask. I release the mistakes of yesterday, and I receive the blessings You have for me today.

In Jesus' name I pray, amen.

ONE

COUNTERFEIT CONVICTIONS

Growing up in Texas, I learned a lot of colorful sayings, many of which I had to abandon when I became a pastor. However, one of those sayings probably applies to you right now: This ain't my first rodeo.

You could fill the bed of a Ford F-150 pickup with all the books and financial articles out there about investing, retirement accounts, saving, mortgages, home buying, and debt. It's probably a safe bet that whenever you flip through a magazine article on finance or look at most books on the topic, you think, *Yeah, I've heard that before.*

This ain't your first rodeo. Wasn't mine either.

As a teenager, I had a subscription to *Money* magazine. I paid cash for my first car. The first home Scott and I purchased as newlyweds had a fifteen-year, fixed-rate mortgage with payments of only $675 a month. We put 10 percent down.

We started out smart, but somewhere along the way, we got stupid. Real stupid.

After only a year, that little house wasn't good enough anymore. So we upgraded, this time with no money down and a thirty-year loan. A traffic accident totaled my paid-for car, so I went into debt to buy another brand-new car, which I quickly tired of and traded in for yet another one.

Credit cards furnished the nicer house and handled any repairs we had not bothered to save up for. Then the baby came.

And so the cycle began.

I had read all the books. I had all the information. And I still made bad choices.

Sound familiar? Chances are, you've made bad choices too. And you knew better.

As a believer in Christ, you have probably read a good bit of the Bible. You may have even read all of it several times. Maybe you're like me and went to one of those Christian schools that made you diagram Bible verses during the sentence structure lessons in English class. Fun, right?

Lack of biblical knowledge, for many Christians, is not the problem. And usually, neither is lack of conviction.

As Christians we have convictions, things we hold to be true, principles we hold in our hearts and endeavor to live out every day. If you were sitting in my office, I could have you read the Great Commission to me out of Matthew 28, and you could probably explain to me, quite passionately, that it means we have a calling to share the good news of Christ with the world. But if we turned back just a few pages and I asked you to read the parable of the talents in Matthew 25, you would probably get a confused look on your face and perhaps give me a Robin Hood analogy, tinged with disgust: "The rich get richer, and the poor get poorer."

Wrong answer.

Let me ask you this: How are you going to spread the good news of Christ all over the world, or fund the work of missionaries who do, if you don't have any *money*? Would God have given us the parable of the talents simply to convey that it's hopeless? I think not.

> How are you going to spread the good news of Christ all over the world, or fund the work of missionaries who do, if you don't have any *money*?

You've certainly read financial books before, along with countless magazine articles about getting your ducks in a row. And you probably beat yourself up for not doing those things you read about. You've read the Bible, you know what you believe, and you've absorbed the common-sense financial stuff. So what's the problem? *What's happening to this information between my eyes, my brain, and my heart?* you wonder. *I read it, I understand it, I agree with it—but I don't do it. Why?*

Ephesians 6:12 explains what we're up against: "We do not wrestle against flesh and blood, but against principalities, against powers, against the rulers of the darkness of this age, against spiritual hosts of wickedness in the heavenly places." Still, I'm not one for giving the devil too much credit. Satan may hand us the rope, but we're the ones who tie the knot and jump off the financial chair.

What happens between the information on the page, the absorption in the brain, and the execution of those ideas in the heart is that *the idea we know we should implement gets polluted by counterfeit convictions.*

Counterfeit convictions are beliefs that started out as biblical truths but that we absorb into our hearts incorrectly. It doesn't matter whether we believe wrongly for selfish reasons, such as deciding that passages on giving and generosity don't apply to us anymore, or for fearful ones, for instance, that God only loves you if you're rich. It also doesn't matter to what degree our convictions are wrong. We can

> **The idea we know we should implement gets polluted by counterfeit convictions.**

be way off base or have an understanding that is skewed just a little bit. And that's all it takes. You don't have to drive your car completely off the freeway to mess up your journey; you can drift just a little bit into the other lane, miss your exit, and ultimately miss your final destination. That's the power of deception. Unfortunately, when we're deceived, we don't know it, and we're often hesitant to acknowledge it when someone else points it out.

A counterfeit conviction, like counterfeit money, looks an awful lot like the real thing. It sometimes takes a trained eye to tell the difference. But if you look closely with a discerning eye, there's always a flaw that gives it away. If we ignore the flaw and try to apply counterfeit convictions to our Christian lives, the results never work out as we expect them to. We end up confused, disappointed, and frustrated with God. Then we get angry because we believe He is not answering our prayers, when in fact, the problem is not with God but with what we've come to expect from Him in our financial woes.

The only weapon against counterfeit convictions is the timeless truths found in God's Word, the Bible. *A timeless truth* is a simple biblical principle that we can count on to lead us down the right path.

> **A timeless truth is a simple biblical principle that we can count on to lead us down the right path.**

If you go back to our counterfeit money analogy, you can put the two terms—*counterfeit convictions* and *timeless truths*—together like this: A counterfeit conviction is like fake money: it looks good, but it's worthless. It may fool some people for a little while, but eventually it will be proved to be what it is: a phony. And just as you can't make a real deposit at a bank with fake money, you can't make a positive impact in your life when your spiritual currency is made up of phony beliefs.

Do you know those penlights cashiers and bank tellers use to verify money's authenticity? That's like a timeless truth. For us, a timeless truth is God's Word and the light of the Holy Spirit shining on our convictions, showing us which ones are real and which ones are phony. *False convictions can't make it past the clarifying light of God's Word.*

Before we go any further, let me be clear about one thing: you are not a bad person if you have counterfeit convictions. Everyone has them. Everyone. All of us at some point in our lives have been duped.

And unfortunately, many of us have been duped in churches, by TV preachers, by friends, by things we have read or seen, by our culture, and even by the devil himself, who the Bible says comes to steal, kill, and destroy (John 10:10). Notice his first dastardly goal is financial in nature—to steal. And not only is he the chief of thieves, he's the father of liars—and he lies to you all the time.

> **False convictions can't make it past the clarifying light of God's Word.**

Have you ever read a promise of God in the Bible and then heard a little whisper that says, "That can't be true! If that were true, you would have that in your life, and you don't! It's a lie!"? That, my friends, is the devil himself, trying to snatch God's promises right out of your heart and your head.

Don't let it happen.

In this book, I'll show you how to avoid having God's promises stolen from you. They're yours to keep, and you should hang on to them for dear life.

While outright lies can be easy to spot—like Monopoly money taken to the grocery store—slight distortions are harder to discern. Those slight distortions of God's truth can come from a million different places: well-meaning friends, misinformed teachers, even pastors with wrong motives. In this book we will walk through simple steps to shine the light on these distortions so their flaws become apparent. It will be like clicking on one of those penlights: examining a conviction against the light of God's Word will reveal it to be either the real deal or phony baloney. And once you know what is real, you simply toss aside what's bad. It's that simple. No guilt, no condemnation, no drama. Just let it go.

Sound easy? It is. It's the lies of the world, the deceit of our materialistic culture, and the influence of selfish people that make things so complicated.

So let's start making them simple.

Shedding Light on the Darkness

Here's an example of a counterfeit conviction and the correlating time-less truth.

Counterfeit Conviction: "I can't really afford this, but I'll just put it on my credit card. When the bill comes, God will provide!"

Timeless Truth: Proverbs 21:17 tells us, "He who loves pleasure will be a poor man; he who loves wine and oil will not be rich."

Temporary pleasures are just that: temporary. They're gone, and then the flesh is off and running, looking for the next cheap thrill. We are only human, after all, and as humans, our fleshly desires can tend to get the better of us from time to time. We must always guard ourselves from chasing the pleasures of stuff because our desires will always outpace our bank balances. Going into debt to fill the bottomless pit of human desire for more and more stuff is a surefire recipe for poverty.

Have some fun, but do so in moderation and within the parameters of a healthy budget. Setting aside some money each month to spend on those impulsive little pleasures lets you have a good time and still meet your financial goals. Spending money is like eating: do it when you have a need, and *occasionally* just because you want to, but never as a medication for pain, loneliness, or disappointment.

That's it.

Did you see how it works? A selfish desire fueled by a lie is squashed by the truth. It's a simple process to unpack these lies; if we don't, we have to live with the fruit of them, which makes our lives very, very complicated. This, my friends, is how Christians get messed up with money.

Once you understand the lies that have led to your bad financial behaviors, you can start addressing them as needed. Some lies are simple to address, such as the one that causes you to overspend when you're bored. Others, like those resulting in spending that is rooted in childhood pain, abandonment issues, past abuse, and other trauma, may take more time to unpack, and you may need professional help. That's okay! Find a trusted pastor or a psychiatrist or psychologist to help you heal from past hurts. You'll do yourself and your counselor a world of good, however, if you can sit down in that first meeting and say, "I'm having financial trouble, and I think it is rooted in this problem." You'll heal more quickly and, if you're paying for counseling, save yourself thousands of dollars in the process.

Understanding Counterfeit Convictions

Now, before you get too comfortable, let me caution you that counterfeit convictions are insidious. They are difficult to identify and even harder to conquer because they are usually based in some sort of truth.

If I told you the sky was purple, you would tell me I was nuts. But if I told you it was blue with just a tinge of purple, and I showed you some really cool video clips while serving a free steak dinner, you might start looking at the sky just a little bit differently.

When I was a newspaper reporter, I once worked on a series of stories about a well-known church revival that was drawing millions of visitors every year and tens of millions of dollars in donations. I attended many services as part of my reporting, and one night I happened to sit next to a prim elderly woman who shared with me her story of why she was there.

She was a widow, and her income was limited to her Social Security checks. She also had health problems that required her to take a number of expensive medications. She had heard that miracles happened at the revival, and she came for hers.

The offering call lasted for more than half an hour.

"Reach into your wallets, and pull out the biggest thing you can find," the pastor told the crowd. He implored everyone in the audience to give at least a hundred dollars—more if possible. Husbands were told to give without consulting their wives. Visiting pastors were told to give from their own churches' budgets, without regard to whether their oversight boards might agree. "God knows how much you have!" the pastor bellowed, reminding the audience that they had spent money on TVs, cars, toys, and clothes.

I watched in disbelief as the widow sitting next to me pulled out a wad of cash.

"This is the money I've set aside for my medicine," she said, leaning into my ear to be heard over the swells of background music.

"Are you sure you want to do that?" I asked.

Her response? "God will provide."

I felt sick. Probably not as sick as she felt later that month without her pills, but sick nonetheless.

That poor woman was sucked in by an emotional, manipulative moment in which she made a decision that under normal circumstances I would venture to guess she would not have made.

During the nightly offering calls, the pastors onstage would cajole the crowds with tales of orphanages funded, souls saved, and lives changed, and pull guilt trips on the crowd over the enormous cost of putting on their nightly show. Yet when another reporter and I asked for confirmation of their spending, we were denied. "It's nobody's business but ours," a staff pastor told us. "We are not accountable to the people who come to revival, because they are our guests. They are making a freewill offering and therefore should not expect an audit or an accounting.

"If you wonder where the money is going," he continued, "then don't give. Obviously, we can't spend money the way people want us to, but once it becomes a gift, it is ours to use. It is nobody's business how we use it."

> **As Christians, we have a responsibility to be good stewards of the money God entrusts to us.**

That statement alone isn't what continues to shock me to this day, more than a decade later. What astounds me is that even after the revival crumbled, the leaders went on to create new ministries and churches, and they continue to collect millions of dollars from well-meaning Christians.

As Christians, we have a responsibility to be good stewards of the money God entrusts to us. If we get suckered in by emotional pleas and fail to do our due diligence into the ministries we consider supporting, we're not helping the kingdom of God; we're just wasting our money.

Search the Scriptures

When the apostle Paul and his buddy Silas went to the town of Berea in Acts 17, they found the people there to be "fair-minded." They based that assessment on the fact that the Bereans "received the word with all readiness and searched the Scriptures daily to find out whether these things were so" (v. 11).

Now, I would think that if any pastor could be taken at his word, it would be Paul. And yet he lauded the Bereans for checking things out by comparing what they received from him to God's Word. That's wisdom.

We have to exercise wisdom. Yet often Christians react to what they are told by some guy in a suit with a microphone without ever holding up those words to the light of Scripture.

Proverbs 2 tells us that "the LORD gives wisdom" (v. 6). It goes on to say, "Discretion will preserve you; understanding will keep you, to deliver you from the way of evil, from the man who speaks perverse things, from those who leave the paths of uprightness" (vv. 11–13). That's a warning that God didn't just put our brains there to keep our ears apart. If the Lord is giving something away, I want it. Don't you? He is giving away wisdom. All we have to do is ask for it and receive it.

"God Will Provide!"

Philippians 4:19 says God will "supply all your need according to His riches in glory by Christ Jesus." In other words, God will provide.

Amen to that! God does provide. And we should give. We will explore biblical giving principles later in this book, but for now, let's revisit my widow friend at the revival and see where things went south for her.

The fallacy in her thinking was that she hung on to "God will provide" without considering the biblical parameters of God's provision.

In Matthew 17, Peter got all stressed out by the guys who came to collect the temple tax. (That's right, even Jesus paid His taxes.) Jesus told Peter to take a chill pill and go fishing. The first fish he caught, Jesus said, would have money in its mouth that Peter could use to pay the taxes.

Now, my elderly friend didn't have to go fishing; her Social Security check was her provision. Out of that, she had wisely set aside money for her prescriptions. And she gave it away.

Can you imagine Peter taking the fish money and giving it to one of the Pharisees for some sermons on tape instead of paying the taxes with it? I would not want to be the one to have to explain *that* move to the Messiah.

You may be wondering how I know that widow squandered her provision, which would inevitably mean she didn't have her medication that month. I don't. I had no way of following up with her, so here's full disclosure that I'm making an assumption here on how her emotionally charged gift turned out.

I will say this, however: I've been blessed in my life to see God move many times in my life and the lives of people around me. And I can say, without a doubt, that when God is involved, there is peace, calm, and the very blessed assurance we sing about in church. What I saw on that woman's face at the revival service that day was fear and panic, and the kind of sickly hope that pours out of manipulation. When you see that kind of grief over an act of giving, you don't need a tweed coat and a magnifying class to figure out that she was probably driven by guilt and fear, not the presence of God. Watching her, I got totally creeped out. My friends, when Jesus is at work, it's never, ever creepy. A discomfort in your spirit is a sign that one of your convictions has been tainted by a lie. And once it's tainted, it becomes counterfeit.

> A discomfort in your spirit is a sign that one of your convictions has been tainted by a lie.

I have no doubt that sweet woman had likely followed Jesus her whole life. She probably came into that revival with some pretty healthy ideas about who He is and how He provides for her. But one thirty-minute offering call was probably enough to skew her ideas about giving and godly provision for the rest of her life when things didn't turn out as she hoped they would. If that gift did not turn into the provision she so desperately needed, she will pause before she gives—every time she gives—for the rest of her life. She will remember that time she did without, and no blessing came.

That is the awesome power of deception.

Understanding how convictions get tainted is the first step toward cleaning up our own hearts, minds, and spirits so we can then tackle the work of cleaning up our finances. And believe me, once you get the junk out of your spirit, getting out of debt and saving for tomorrow is a cakewalk by comparison.

Misunderstanding and Misapplication of Scripture

You probably know people who like to spew Bible verses to fit their every need. Those people are annoying, aren't they? The problem is that most Christians only read the Bible on Sunday morning, and they only read the verses the pastor uses in his sermon. That's certainly better than nothing, but it's not giving you the full picture.

Hebrews 4:12 says, "The Word of God is living and powerful and sharper than any two-edged sword." I don't know any good sword analogies, so let me put it to you this way: not taking the time to read and understand the Bible, to pray its promises over your life and your family, and to seize the power that lies within it is like walking to work when you have a Porsche in the driveway. You may eventually get to your office, but when you do, you will be tired, dirty, and too strung out to get any real work done. And that's if you make it and don't get flattened by a truck on the way. The alternative, of course, is slipping into a leather seat, putting that sweet ride in gear, and speeding along with songs from your iPod spilling out of the perfectly tuned speakers.

Drive the Porsche, my friends.

Not understanding the Bible in its full context leaves you open to manipulation by people who use the Scriptures to fit their purposes, instead of to bring truth. As an adult and a Christian, you have to take responsibility for what seeps into your brain and settles in your heart. Taking what some guy on TV tells you at face value without "searching the Scriptures daily to find out whether these things are so" is lazy. If you have to be spoon-fed your belief system, and you refuse to engage your brain, then you should expect to get taken advantage of, ripped off, and manipulated.

> Not understanding the Bible in its full context leaves you open to manipulation by people who use the Scriptures to fit their purposes, instead of to bring truth.

And many Christians settle for exactly that.

Imagine some guy on TV telling you to clean out your savings account and send the proceeds to him. Not such a far-fetched scenario, believe me. In his pitch he reads Luke 6:38: "Give, and it will be given to you; good measure, pressed down, shaken together, and running over will be put into your bosom. For with the same measure that you use, it will be measured back to you."

Great scripture, and I believe it. However, go back a few hundred pages to the story of Joseph and how he stored up in the seven years of plenty for the seven years of famine. (Of course, the New Testament wasn't around when Joseph was running things, but let's give God credit for knowing this whole book-of-Luke thing was coming around eventually.) If Joseph had given away the contents of the storehouses on a whim, the people of his day would have starved during the famine. Instead, he followed God's orders and prepared ahead.

Don't get me wrong: I know people who have given extravagantly and abundantly and were extremely blessed by it. I even know someone who once gave away everything he owned. But those people heard God, prayed through what they heard (believe me, they prayed!), sought wise counsel from other Christians and their pastor, and knew where their gifts were going. They didn't make a rash, emotional decision based on the teary appeal of some guy on TV.

What's more, the people who gave away things actually *owned* the things they gave away. You can't give away a car to a single mom in need if you still have to make payments on it, and you can't give away a mortgaged house. And I don't know of anyone who was blessed for giving an extravagant cash gift when they had credit card debt. And I sure don't know any wise or supernaturally blessed people who ever put an extravagant gift *on* a credit card. However, I see broke people charging their "tithe" all the time because they already spent all their paycheck. (Here's a hint: if it's not your money, you're not really giving! You think the people at Visa need your blessings? Well, maybe they do, but don't you need these blessings too?)

People who are only after your money spew out Scriptures presenting God as some sort of supernatural ATM who will open the windows of heaven over you if you funnel your cash to a certain televangelist. God does bless us according to the level of generosity we have in our hearts. But He looks at more than amounts; He looks at intention. He examines our hearts. Give with a stingy heart and wrong intentions and you won't like the results.

> **Give with a stingy heart and wrong intentions and you won't like the results.**

Here's another often misapplied Bible verse from Matthew 6: "Do not worry about tomorrow, for tomorrow will worry about its own things. Sufficient for the day is its own trouble." People have quoted that verse to me as justification for not saving any money. They can have not two shiny dimes set aside for retirement and still give me smug righteousness and a lecture on faith when I ask them why.

Here we get back to the importance of reading the *whole* book, folks.

Proverbs 21:20 says, "In the house of the wise are stores of choice food and oil, but *a foolish man devours all he has*" (emphasis added). That sounds a lot like a person with a big plasma TV but no 401(k) to me.

None of us will ever understand the entire Bible. But we have a responsibility to ourselves to try to get as much out of it as we can. If you don't understand something, ask your pastor, Bible study leader, or a trusted and wise Christian friend. Get a good concordance and some study guides. Pray about it. Engage that brain of yours.

Guilt and Condemnation

Another root of counterfeit convictions is the toxic cocktail of guilt and condemnation. These happen to be strong gifts of many religious groups, and most of all, my dear Southern Baptist grandmother (may she rest in peace in the arms of our heavenly Father), who could guilt ya with the best of them.

To fully understand guilt and condemnation, first, let's explore the difference between condemnation and conviction. Condemnation makes you feel marked as a bad person and a failure because of something you have done, said, or believed. Conviction is a stirring in your heart that compels you to examine a thought, action, or belief and *challenges you* to repent and do better next time.

Convictions are good. Condemnation is bad.

You don't see this Scripture held up at football games, but it's almost as important as the one it follows: John 3:17 says that "God did not send His Son into the world to condemn the world, but that the world through Him might be saved." When we feel guilty and condemned, we easily make foolish choices with our money in an effort to "buy" the pain away. Divorced parents can be experts at this. Regardless of whether they had any control over the circumstances that led to the ending of the marriage, divorced parents tend to compensate for the breakup of the family by throwing money at their kids' pain. We've all seen it, but have you ever seen it work? It backfires pretty much every time.

Guilt can also make an otherwise perfectly rational adult ignore perfectly rational needs—for example, saving for your kids' college education while ignoring your retirement account is a first-class exercise in stupidity. Many parents think that by sacrificing their own needs to provide for their children, they're being better parents. But unless you plan on burning Junior's diploma to keep the house warm in your old age, you are not being good to your kids or yourself.

And I want to free you right now from any guilt that may have been thrust upon you by any pastors who chastise their congregations for having homes and cars and televisions. I've heard it more than I care to recall. Are we all supposed to live in tent camps in the church parking lot? If that's what you feel led to do, well, more power to you. Personally, I don't think that brings much glory to God, although it may result in a few more options on your pastor's Lexus.

One televangelist, while not outright criticizing viewers for having food in their pantries, did notably praise all the sweet little ladies who gave their grocery money to support that particular TV ministry. I have to wonder . . . when those sweet little ladies ended up in line at the local food pantry so they didn't starve to death, did that bring honor and glory to God?

> **If your pastor continually tries to make you feel bad so you give more, find another church.**

Don't get me wrong. I believe we should give generously to our churches, and as a pastor, I believe they should be well supported. I believe Christians should tithe (again, more on that later). But making people feel bad in an attempt to manipulate them to give more is just plain wrong, and it robs the congregation of the blessing they get from giving—you can't feel happy and satisfied in your giving if you've given because someone twisted your arm. That's not generosity; it's coercion, and it is fun for no one.

Second Corinthians 9:7 says, "Let each one give as he purposes in his heart, not grudgingly or of necessity; for God loves a *cheerful* giver" (emphasis added). If your pastor continually tries to make you feel bad so you give more, find another church.

Guilt and condemnation can also creep in when we are unsure of our salvation or of who we are in Christ. Galatians 3:26 says that we are all "sons of God through faith in Christ Jesus." But not all Christians believe it.

The senior pastor of my church, Brady Boyd, says that Christians can be broken down into three groups: orphans, slaves, and sons and daughters. Orphans are always unsure of their place in the family and don't believe they really belong. They often wander through life with no sense of purpose and find it difficult to commit long-term to a career, a marriage, or a ministry assignment. Orphans have a hard time trusting people and will tend to hurt others before they get hurt themselves.

Slaves know they have an assignment but are convinced the only way to please the father is to perform and work harder than others. Their place in the family is dependent on how well they do something.

Real freedom can only come through accepting your place as a son or daughter in God's kingdom. Sons know they have chores and assignments, but they also know that the father is more pleased with who they are becoming than what they are doing,

Think of how that applies to our money. Someone who feels like an orphan in Christ will be fear based and reluctant to give. He will hoard his money. A person with a slave mentality may try to buy favor, using money as a manipulation tool. Only someone who accepts his or her place as a son or daughter of God can feel free to make wise financial decisions—to give, save, meet current needs, and plan for the future—with enough left over for today.

God's Word Versus My Will

Never underestimate the influence of a person's will on her ability to twist and bend the "rules" to fit her circumstances. Don't believe me? Just watch any woman worth her salt justify a designer handbag purchase. Personally, I am a pro.

My all-time best example of my ability to shift the very fabric of financial prudence to fit my current obsession was when I decided we needed an RV. Now, we had never owned one, never been in one, and knew nothing about them, but for some reason I believed this was all we needed to make our lives complete. Follow me, if you will, through my circular maze of logic to justify the purchase of a twenty-three-thousand-dollar, twenty-eight-foot travel trailer, complete with stainless-steel appliances, two queen-sized beds, and every gizmo under the sun.

1. Our three-year-old son had a God-given right to go camping, catch bugs, and roast marshmallows under the stars. As his mother, I had a God-given right to do it in style.
2. It would enable us to have more family time. (Any argument on this point made my opponent vulnerable to accusations of not caring about "family time.")
3. I wanted it.
4. All other arguments referred to #3.

Now my husband's arguments against the purchase:

1. We knew nothing about RVs and would likely careen off a cliff while trying to tow the stupid thing during "family time."
2. We really couldn't afford it, even with "easy monthly payments" of "only" $235 a month.
3. All other arguments referred to #2.

My friends, I'm not proud of this, but when it appeared that for the first time in my young marriage, I might not get my way, I threw a bit of a tempter tantrum. I was so mad and so convinced of my husband's lack of love for me and concern for my happiness and that of our son that I actually slept on the couch.

Scott relented, and we bought the stupid thing. We took it out exactly six times before we had to sell it because we moved to Texas. It sat on a consignment lot for fifteen months before it finally sold at a loss of $3,500, not counting all those "easy" $235 payments we had made since the initial purchase. For that much money, we could have gone to Europe. First class. Twice.

I'm happy to report that my husband did not leave me. In fact, he's such a saint that he never even brings it up. But I remember this as a clear example to myself and anyone around me that my will can be a very dangerous thing. I bet yours can be too.

Luke 14:28–29 says, "Which of you, intending to build a tower, does not sit down first and count the cost, whether he has enough to finish it—lest, after he has laid the foundation and is not able to finish, all who see it begin to mock him." In other words, where buying is concerned, if you don't push your selfish wants out of the way to see what the purchase is actually going to cost, you risk having every Bible study group you ever attend for the rest of your life interrupted with demands to tell the new couple "that funny story about all the money you wasted on the RV." That's not what I want to be known for, people.

Now that you know what counterfeit convictions are and how they can lurk undetected in our spirits, the real work begins. In the chapters ahead, we're going to explore some of the most common reasons why Christians fail with money. We're going to root out your own personal counterfeit convictions, toss them out, and prepare you to break your bad money habits once and for all.

Let's ask God to show us His truth in His Word in His timing. Pray this out loud:

Father God, I acknowledge that my current financial habits may be inconsistent with what Your Word teaches because my current financial condition does not line up with the promises of the Bible. God, open my heart and my mind to new ideas and fresh thinking. Help me to see what You want me to see, when You want me to see it. Father, bless my efforts to become financially healthy, and let my decisions bless my family and honor You.

In Jesus' name I pray. Amen.

God's Way

Here are the most important points to take away from chapter 1.

- Counterfeit convictions are beliefs that started out as biblical truths but we absorbed incorrectly into our hearts.
- For most Christians, lack of biblical knowledge isn't what keeps us from doing what the Bible says about money. The problem is that the ideas we know we should implement get polluted by counterfeit convictions.
- A timeless truth is a simple biblical principle that we can count on to lead us down the right path.
- False convictions can't make it past the clarifying light of God's Word.
- As Christians, we have a responsibility to be good stewards of the money God entrusts to us.
- The Bible teaches that it is wise to compare what we are taught to God's Word, to ensure that we are being taught good principles.
- A discomfort in your spirit is a sign that one of your convictions has been tainted by a lie.
- Not understanding the Bible in its full context leaves you open to manipulation by people who use the Scriptures to fit their purposes, instead of to bring truth.
- We must guard our hearts against people who use manipulation and false teaching to get people to give to their ministries. God wants us to give out of grateful hearts, not out of fear and manipulation.
- Convictions are good. Condemnation is bad.

Solution Steps

Here are simple steps you and your family can take today to help you improve your relationship with God and do better with your money.

1. Make a list of the things you know you should be doing with your money but that you're not currently doing. Beside each item, list a couple of reasons why you're not doing what you wish you were. Refer to this list as you read through this book, and note which counterfeit convictions might be preventing you from achieving financial success.

2. Name three really smart things you've done with your finances. Did you open up a 401(k)? Or shop around for a great deal on your mortgage? Did you pay cash for your car? Do you have a good cash cushion in your emergency fund? Next to each item on your list, describe the attitudes and behaviors that led you to make those smart decisions. How can you carry this conduct over to other areas of your financial life?

3. If you had a bottomless bank account, how would you expand God's kingdom with your resources? What would you like to do with extra money, and what do you think God would have you do to bless others? Write down your thoughts as you explore the question of God's greater financial purpose for your life. What are some things you could do now with the resources you currently have? Having a wish list of what you would like to do with extra money someday or even now will keep you focused on your values and your purpose when spending urges might otherwise derail your plans.

4. Have you ever believed something about the Bible and then later, through personal study or through teaching, discovered that what you previously believed was wrong? Make a list of beliefs you've had that were later proved wrong or that changed somehow. How many of those beliefs would you classify as counterfeit convictions that negatively affected your behavior, prayer life, or relationship with God? Take a few moments to write down how you felt when you realized you needed to change your thinking, and the kind of teaching or Bible study that helps you see God's Word more

clearly. Do you grow in your spiritual life most effectively through Sunday sermons, private prayer and study, Bible study group discussions, or in a different way altogether?

5. Make a list of some of the things you do or buy when you need a little pick-me-up. Are these things good for you, bad for you, or neutral? Are there ways you could perk up your day without spending money? How long do these pleasures last for you?

6. List three beliefs or behaviors concerning money that you would like to change. Does money burn a hole in your pocket and you wish you could save more? Do you hoard money out of fear that you might not have enough someday? List the things you want to change, and pray now that as you read this book, God will help you understand His will for you in those areas.

7. As you go through the remaining chapters, highlight in your Bible the passages that are reviewed. This will provide a quick reference to enable you to do as the Bereans did and "search the Scriptures daily to find out whether these things [are] so" (Acts 17:11).

Two

THE FIX-IT FANTASY

It's amazing the power we ascribe to a dollar bill. Accumulate enough of them and—POW!—suddenly we think we're more popular, attractive, healthy, intelligent, and secure. The more money we have, the better—or more evil, depending on our perspective—we believe we are as people. Money not only holds the very power of good and evil within its linen and cotton fibers, we think, but money *is* power.

Money is not power. It's not transformative. It doesn't change who you are. It is just money. So why are so many of us messed up over it?

The Bible talks about money and possessions more than any other topic except love. Think about that for a moment: it is the second most popular topic in the *entire Bible*. Why? I think there are two reasons: First, God knew most of us would struggle with having the right attitude about money and possessions. Second, the way we handle money reveals the condition of our hearts.

One of the fundamental principles of my ministry at our church stems from the teaching in Matthew 6:25–33:

Do not worry about your life, what you will eat or what you will drink; nor about your body, what you will put on. Is not life more than food and the body more than clothing? Look at the birds of the air, for they neither sow nor reap nor gather into barns, yet your heavenly Father feeds them. Are you not of more value than they?

Which of you by worrying can add one cubit to his stature? So why do you worry about clothing? Consider the lilies of the field, how they grow; they neither toil nor spin; and yet I say to you that even Solomon in all his glory was not arrayed like one of these.

Now if God so clothes the grass of the field, which today is, and tomorrow is thrown into the oven, will He not much more clothe you, O you of little faith? Therefore do not worry, saying, "What shall we eat?" or "What shall we drink?" or "What shall we wear?" For after all these things the Gentiles seek. For your heavenly Father knows that you need all these things. But seek first the kingdom of God and His righteousness, and all these things shall be added to you.

I firmly believe that it is God's will for His people to live without financial stress and worry. And we can get closer to God by taking the time to understand His role in our finances. We can also get closer to Him by understanding *our* role in our finances.

> **It is God's will for His people to live without financial stress and worry.**

Because God has promised to provide for our every need, I believe that financial problems are never inherently about money, but are instead usually symptoms of underlying spiritual problems.

Counterfeit Conviction: Money has the power to fix me and my problems.

Timeless Truth: People with more money don't have fewer problems, they just have different problems. And people with more money don't have fewer personal issues, they just have different issues.

Neither having more money nor having none at all is necessarily symptomatic of God's blessings on our lives, His favor, or our ability to get into heaven. Having money with the right attitude and a pure, grateful heart is living a blessed life. So is living with humble means and the right attitude and a pure, grateful heart.

Deuteronomy 8:18 says, "Remember the LORD your God, for it is He who gives you power to get wealth." In the parable of the talents in Matthew 25:14–29, Jesus made it clear that some of us would exercise that "power to get wealth" more effectively than others.

In the parable of the "talents" (a measure of money), Jesus compared the kingdom of God to a wealthy man who entrusted to three different servants varied amounts of cash, "each according to his ability" (v. 15). The servant who received the most money did the best with it: through trading, he doubled his already significant wealth. So did the guy who received the second-largest amount.

But the servant who received the least amount of money was fearful, and instead of investing the money, he buried it so he wouldn't lose it. He then told his master, "Lord, I knew you to be a hard man, reaping where you have not sown, and gathering where you have not scattered seed. And I was afraid, and went and hid your talent in the ground. Look, there you have what is yours" (vv. 24–25).

The wealthy man called his servant "wicked and lazy" for not at least putting the money in the bank so it could earn some interest (v. 26). And he took that servant's wealth and gave it to the first guy, who had been given the most to begin with.

It's worth noting here the comments of the "wicked and lazy" servant. What can we surmise by what he said to his master? He feared his master, but not in a respectful way. He called his master a "hard man," essentially accusing him of being a thief and a bully. Who does that instantly bring to mind? Certainly not God, who could never be a thief or a bully and is surely not "hard" toward us, or He would not have sacrificed His Son to save a fallen world. If the servant's words were reflective of his experience with his earthly master, we have to assume the other two servants saw the same thing because all three had the same master. But the other two didn't let fear shut them down, did they? Only the third servant was wicked and lazy, because he tied his anticipation of financial success to the actions of a flawed master and a harsh world. How often do we let fear undermine our success, even allowing it to rule us? How often do we duck and run for cover when we have a setback?

> **How often do we let fear undermine our success?**

Jesus said very clearly that He wants us to do very well with what we have, so we can be entrusted with more. And not so we can build wealth just for the sake of getting rich but so that we can care for our families, leave an inheritance to our grandchildren, and take care of the poor, or in this case, the ones who buried their money in the ground.

Jesus loves the poor. He doesn't fault them, and He even commands the wealthy to care for them. But He also understands that when it comes to money and wealth building, some of us are going to get it, and some of us aren't.

Wealth building is both a talent and a skill. You can be born with a gift for managing money, but even if you're not, you can certainly develop money-management skills. Yet doing so doesn't make you inherently a better person, just a wealthier one. Still, most Christians have very strong opinions about what more or less money will do to their identities and even their souls. Here are some examples.

Money Will Make Me a Bad Person

Many Christians think poverty is a sign of spiritual purity. And some scriptures, if not taken in the context of *everything* the Bible teaches about money and wealth, might seem to support such a belief. In Luke 9:23, Jesus said, "If anyone desires to come after Me, let him deny himself, and take up his cross daily, and follow Me."

Each of us is to live a life that pursues Christ. We are not to exist solely to indulge in the meaningless pleasures of the world. We must seek to honor and glorify God by caring for those in need. But there is a difference in building wealth for the sake of building wealth or for personal indulgence and building it for the sake of helping others in Jesus' name. On the other hand, being poor for the sake of being poor is no more Christlike than getting rich for the sake of getting rich. We have to strive for balance.

> **Being poor for the sake of being poor is no more Christlike than getting rich for the sake of getting rich. We have to strive for balance.**

There are three types of people with a poverty mentality: (1) those who consciously avoid building any kind of wealth because they think it will make them evil; (2) those who think they're struggling financially because God is mad at them or has cursed them; and (3) those who manage their money poorly and find piety in their self-imposed poverty.

All are wrong ways of thinking.

It takes money to help the poor, to buy vaccines for children in third-world countries, to build clinics and dig water wells, and to send missionaries to faraway lands to spread the good news of Christ. Jesus commanded us to do all of these things, but we can't do them without money. As Margaret Thatcher once said, "No one would remember the good Samaritan if he'd only had good intentions. He had money as well."

Another passage that wrongly feeds a poverty mentality is Matthew 19:24: "It is easier for a camel to go through the eye of a needle than for a rich man to enter the kingdom of God." Those words confounded even the disciples, who asked, "Who then can be saved?" Jesus answered, "With men this is impossible, but with God, all things are possible" (vv. 25–26).

This is fascinating to explore. When you take verse 24 and compare it to the parable of the talents, at first, it appears to be a contradiction, but it's not. Consider this: in the parable, the wealthy man didn't *give* his money to the servants; he entrusted it to them for a time, because he was going out of town. In the same way, God has made it clear in His Word that, though He owns everything in the world, He entrusts a portion of His wealth to us. It is still His; we just have an opportunity to do something great with it.

Another reason these passages support each other is that in the parable, the two "good and faithful" servants were multiplying their master's money *on his behalf.* They didn't keep it for themselves; they doubled their money and returned both portions back to their master. Contrast that with wealth-building American-style. We either build wealth to buy nicer houses, flashier cars, and fancier clothes, or we blow it all and go into debt to maintain the illusion of wealth. That's not representative of the kingdom of God. Jesus knew it would be difficult for the rich to enter God's kingdom because so many of them built their wealth with a tainted worldview.

Here are two more scriptures, both from Luke 12, often used to justify a poverty mentality:

First there is the parable of the rich fool in verses 16–21, where a rich man decided to build bigger barns to hold all of his stuff, so he could retire in a hammock, drink in hand. The passage ends with these words: "'Fool! This night your soul will be required of you; then whose will those things be which you have provided?' So is he who lays up treasure for himself, and is not rich toward God."

Verses 33 and 34 tell us what he should have done: "Sell what you have and give alms; provide yourselves money bags which do not grow old, a treasure in the heavens that does not fail, where no thief approaches nor moth destroys. For where your treasure is, there your heart will be also." Yet the rich fool accumulated stuff for the sake of accumulating stuff. He did not have his eyes on God or on helping his fellow man. He only had eyes for that hammock. And while the other passage doesn't explicitly spell this out, how can you sell things to help the poor when you never accumulated anything to *sell* in the first place?

I'm sure you've heard the apostle Paul being quoted as saying, "Money is the root of all evil." But actually, that's not what he said. In

1 Timothy 6:10, Paul said, "*The love of* money is *a* root of all kinds of evil, from which *some* have strayed from the faith in their greediness" (emphasis added). In other words, greed and money-loving cause some otherwise faithful people to stumble. So should we take this and those other scriptures I've outlined here to mean that money is bad and to be avoided? Of course not. We just have to handle it with care; keep our wallets open to those in need; and keep our eyes, minds, and hearts on God.

Money Will Make Me Happy

How many times have you heard various versions of this lie? How often have you believed it yourself, saying things like, "If I just made another five thousand dollars a year, everything would be okay" or, "If we could just have that house, life would be perfect"? Have you ever met a truly happy person and thought, *Yeah, if I made as much as that guy makes, I would be happy too?*

> If you're not grateful for what you have now, you won't be grateful with more.

Again this goes back to being "faithful with little." If you're not grateful for what you have now, you won't be grateful with more. In 1 Timothy 6:6 the apostle Paul wrote, "Godliness with *contentment* is great gain" (emphasis added). And he mentioned contentment again in his letter to the Philippian church: "I have learned in whatever state I am, to be content. I know how to be abased, and I know how to abound. Everywhere and in all things I have learned both to be full and to be hungry, both to abound and to suffer need. I can do all things through Christ who strengthens me" (4:11–13). The last sentence from this passage is often used by Christian coaches to encourage players on sports teams. But the original context of this passage is important: we can endure all financial situations through *the power of Christ*, who lives within us and strengthens us. Without His help, how likely are we to just fall into a state of contentment on our own? Contentment requires prayer and perseverance. We have to ask Jesus to help us be content with where we are and with what we have.

What if we paused for a moment and asked ourselves why we really want that bigger television. Why can't we be content with the one that is there now, as long as it is work-ing decently? Why can't we be grateful for the functional car that gets us back and forth to work every day instead of lusting over the neighbors' new SUV? Why is it always more, more, more?

> We have to ask Jesus to help us be content with where we are and with what we have.

When we ask those questions, God will bless our pursuit of contentment.

A few years ago, Scott and I decided to try to find ways we could leave behind the more, more, more and pursue ways to have less, less, less. It's become a regular practice for us to have discussions about whether we really want something that we think we want—or if we just want it because it's there. My favorite example of this is sitting in our garage right now.

Our move to Colorado dramatically changed our lifestyle in sig-nificant ways. Instead of both of us commuting thirty minutes or more each way to work every day in the Dallas–Fort Worth area, Scott was able to start working from home. And because we lived a mere three minutes from the church where I worked, my commute became negligible. The kids' new school was just a few blocks away from our new house. Suddenly, a Texas-sized commute was no longer part of our day, praise God.

While I was grateful for this change, I did not give a whole lot of thought to it until a certain coaching session opened my eyes to some-thing new.

One of the things I pride myself on in my ministry and in coach-ing families through financial problems is that I never ask others to do something I either have not done or am not willing to do myself. One day, I was telling a couple that they could get rid of their second car, and as the words were coming out of my mouth, I felt a little nudge from the Holy Spirit.

Are you *willing to give up* your *second car?*

Ouch.

That night I discussed our car situation with Scott. We had a relatively new crossover-type SUV we had purchased in Texas shortly before we moved to Colorado. It was not four-wheel drive, and I had already slid off the road once in the snow and ruined my tires from slamming into a curb. We had a lot of debt on that car.

Our other car was Scott's paid-for, twelve-year-old Honda Civic that miraculously only had 80,000 miles on it, but was even more useless in the Colorado snow than my crossover SUV.

What if we sold both cars and bought one good-quality used car that would handle the snow better and reduce our debt?

What a plan! We now save hundreds a year on car insurance, gas, and maintenance. We significantly reduced our car debt, which we expect to fully eliminate in short order. We saved the time and headaches of maintaining a second car, and we have lots more room now in the garage. All from having less.

Sometimes, less truly is more.

I've already mentioned this scripture, but it bears repeating. Proverbs 21:17 says, "He who loves pleasure will be a poor man." Most of us define pleasure as coming from temporary things: a new flat-screen television, a massage, a beach vacation. Those things are nice, but they certainly don't create long-term happiness. Trying to find our happiness in "stuff" is a recipe for misery. When we are always striving for the next thing on our list, we will always be striving. It never ends. There is always something newer, bigger, better, faster, and shinier. Proverbs 27:20 says, "The eyes of man are never satisfied." That was written by King Solomon, the wisest man who ever lived. He was also the richest man who ever lived, and he had seven

> Trying to find our happiness in "stuff" is a recipe for misery.

hundred wives and three hundred mistresses. Pleasure in any form (well, except HDTV, of course) was available to Solomon twenty-four hours a day. Yet a man known throughout history for having it all also wrote these words in Ecclesiastes 12:13, "Let us hear the conclusion of the whole matter: Fear God and keep His commandments. For this is man's all." In everything Solomon had, he found his greatest joys when he was closest to God, and his greatest sorrows and losses when he turned away from God. You can read about Solomon's downfall in 1 Kings 11.

None of us can be wealthier than Solomon or have more wisdom, so how can we expect a different result when we chase stuff to make us happy?

Here's another golden verse from Luke 12: verse 15 says, "One's life does not consist in the abundance of the things he possesses." My grandmother used to put it this way: "More stuff means more stuff to dust."

And if you've ever heard of the "lottery curse," you've seen this principle play out in many modern lives as well. You can Google the term for a laundry list of examples where people's lives have been ruined by winning the lottery. And often, the bigger the prize, the bigger the downfall. Big money comes with big responsibilities that most winners are not equipped to handle.

Money Will Make Me Safe

This one is a doozy.

Putting our trust in how much money we have in the bank is a surefire formula for unhappiness. Banks go under. Stocks crash. Real estate values can plummet.

I have a close friend who made a killing in a real estate deal in 2000. He socked the cash away into some stocks and thought he was set. The stocks he picked? Enron, airlines, and tech. As Homer Simpson

> Putting our trust in how much money we have in the bank is a surefire formula for unhappiness.

would say, "D'oh!" Fortunately, my friend also has a good sense of humor, and he chalked his losses up to experience and moved on.

In Psalm 37:3–4 King David wrote, "Trust in the LORD, and do good; dwell in the land, and feed on His faithfulness. Delight yourself also in the LORD, and He shall give you the desires of your heart." We are to be good stewards, invest wisely, build up our resources, but put our *trust* in God and only God. Our blessings come from Him, not from our bank accounts. "Feed on His faithfulness" for a kind of nourishment for your soul that you cannot get by watching the stock market. "Delight in the LORD" for a peace that will sustain you when home values fall. And trust that, according to Jeremiah 29:11, God always has a plan to prosper you and not to harm you, to give you hope and a future. Trust means having faith that God's plans are always for our good. That doesn't mean there won't be bumps in the road, because surely, there will be. But bumps are temporary. We can face those setbacks with faith or with fear. Fear causes us to make irrational decisions that may undermine our financial success.

In the past year I've had at least a dozen conversations with people that have gone something like this:

"The value of my home has fallen by 10 percent! What am I going to do?" asks the panicked homeowner.

"Well, that depends," I say. "How soon do you need to sell your home, and why do you have to sell it?"

"Oh, I don't have to sell," they say.

"Then why in the world do you care?" is my response.

Whatever goes up must come down. And vice versa. I've talked to many, many people who panicked and cashed out stocks that have since recouped much if not all of their original value. I've also coached several people who sold their homes simply out of fear that the housing market would tank further. And I've prayed with many older folks who are facing retirement, and even though their portfolios may have years to increase in value, they lie awake at night, wondering if they're going to have to be greeters at Wal-Mart.

It's not that financial losses are a walk in the park; it's just that many of us overreact in fear instead of responding thoughtfully with faith. Fear is an easy reaction to have when your trust is in your bank balance. But when your trust is in almighty God, it's easier to see that God can bless you and care for you no matter what the economy is doing.

Remember: He's seen it all, and He's not worried.

"Whoever trusts in the LORD shall be safe," is the promise of Proverbs 29:25. So even when we think the solution to a problem is money, the solution is always, in fact, God.

If there was ever someone who had reason to believe that safety could come in the form of money, it was the widow who sought the prophet Elisha's help in 2 Kings 4. She owed some money that she could not repay, and in those times, that meant the creditor could take her two sons into slavery. That was just about to happen when she appealed to Elisha for help.

> **Even when we think the solution to a problem is money, the solution is always, in fact, God.**

Now, Elisha didn't pull out a wad of cash to pay off the debt. One has to think if that was God's will, he certainly could have done so. Lots of miracles went through Elisha's hands, after all. But instead he asked the widow to gather jars from her neighbors and begin pouring what little oil she had into them. She did as she was told, although I'm sure it made absolutely no sense to her at the time. And through her obedience, God performed a miracle: as she began filling the jars with the small amount that she had, the oil lasted until the last jar was full.

"Go sell the oil and pay your debt," Elisha instructed her, "and you and your sons live on the rest" (v. 7). Her sons' freedom and their future livelihood came out of her obedience, which produced a miracle from God.

Most of us aren't facing something as terrible as the loss of our children over our debts or other financial troubles—so why can't we find our safety in God during the storm?

Money Will Make Me Problem Free!

Have you thought about what you would do if you suddenly inherited or won a million dollars? Or five million? Or ten million? Have you ever thought, *If I just had* this *much money, I could pay off all my debts, pay off my mortgage, buy a nice car, and retire worry free*? It's in our nature to think that with enough money, all of our problems will just go away. But like the Notorious B.I.G. song "Mo Money Mo Problems," usually it's a case of "The more money we come across, the more problems we see." As the Beatles sang, "I don't care too much for money. Money can't buy me love."

Once we start focusing on what money could do for us, we stop looking for God's plans for our lives. You can worship the power of money or you can worship God, but Matthew 6:24 says you must choose: you cannot worship God and Money at the same time.

> **You cannot worship God and money at the same time.**

In America, especially, this tends to be true because what happens as soon as we get an increase in income? We upgrade our lifestyle. And the more stuff we have, the more stuff we have to maintain. And the more our kids expect. And the busier we get trying to keep up with it all. And the unhappier we become.

Money could pay off your debts, but then what? If you haven't learned to live below your means, you'll just max out those credit cards all over again. Ask anyone who's cashed out his 401(k) to pay off his debt how well that worked out for him. Most end up in even more debt than they had before they drained their retirement accounts.

Money won't save your marriage, make your children respect you, or win you more friends. It may buy you a nicer house, but not the love to make it a home. And it can buy you a nice vacation, but not true rest or peace.

I've touched on this point already, but it truly is a case of being faithful with little. God's not going to trust you with a lot if you're not effectively managing what He has already blessed you with. The sooner you give up on the notion that more money is the answer to your problems, the closer you will be to finding *true* solutions to what concerns you.

The Three Things You're Not Allowed to Say

I hear a lot of ridiculous, negative comments in my office. Some of the more common include:

"I'll never get out of debt."

"Every time I put money in savings, something happens and I have to take it out. Why bother?"

"We just don't make enough money."

"I can't!"

"If only . . ."

"We had no choice."

I've threatened to make T-shirts imprinted with all of these comments. My best sellers would be the last three. I've heard them so much that they're now the only three things no one is allowed to say in my office. Instead, I teach:

There is always a way.

All we can do is the best we can with the challenges that are before us today.

We always have a choice.

The fact is, our words have a tremendous amount of power over our lives. What we speak has the power to become what we actually experience. Proverbs 18:21 says, "Death and life are in the power of the tongue. And those who love it will eat its fruit." So if you love talking about how broke you are, I seriously hope you enjoy reaping

> **The fact is, our words have a tremendous amount of power over our lives.**

the harvest of your words. Because when you constantly plant those ugly seeds instead of sweet fruits, they will grow up into nasty weeds that you don't want in your life's garden.

> **If God *Himself* is thinking good things about you, what harm is there in doing the same?**

Most of the people I coach have a toxic habit of speaking ill about their finances, their jobs, their marriages, their futures, and their potential. They go on and on about how broke they are and the obstacles they face. And many can get downright combative when I try to lead them into a conversation about the positive things they have going for them, their potential, and the better days ahead that God has for their future. "I know the thoughts I think toward you," God tells us In Jeremiah 29:11, "Thoughts of peace and not of evil, to give you a future and a hope." If you're thinking and speaking negatively about yourself, your life, and your finances, consider this: if God *Himself* is thinking good things about you, what harm is there in doing the same?

Thinking and speaking poverty over your life is indicative of counterfeit convictions and toxic beliefs:

Counterfeit Conviction: I am poor, and that's just how it is. My life has about as much value and potential as my bank account, and that isn't much!

Timeless Truth: You can be broke without being poor. Being poor is a state of mind.

Understand that there is a difference between a poverty mentality and being in a state of thoughtless denial, otherwise known as "word of faith" or "name it and claim it" theology. This belief system dictates that you never admit to being sick, being in debt, or having a need. You should always deny that those states exist, even when you're living in the midst of them.

But that's lying, isn't it?

According to this twisted theology, if someone asks you if you're sick, you should deny it, even if you have snot running out of your nose and you're sneezing like a pepper farmer.

As I write this, I have the flu. I'm not going to walk around the church, bemoaning my fate as a "sick person." I'm not a "sick person," I just happen to have the flu. I won't deny that I have the flu. And at the same time, I am going to believe that God is going to heal me, and I am going to help Him in that process by getting lots of rest, drinking plenty of water, and taking copious amounts of DayQuil and vitamins. Does that mean I have no faith for healing? No, it means I'm going to make it through my workday.

Likewise, if you are experiencing a financial setback, it's okay to acknowledge that you're in a bit of a rough patch. But instead of complaining "I'm so poor! I'm so broke!" simply take stock of your current financial circumstances and devise a plan to turn those circumstances around as soon as possible. *See your setback as a temporary circumstance and not a permanent condition.* God will bless your efforts to get financially healthy, just as you will get a physical healing more quickly if you take good care of yourself.

> **See your setback as a temporary circumstance and not a permanent condition.**

Getting rid of stinkin' thinkin' takes more than just deciding that you're going to "try to be more positive." You have to fight fire with fire. If negative thoughts and words are making your heart and mind feel toxic, you need to clean out the yucky stuff by refusing to entertain negative thoughts or speak negative words. You have to actively choose to think and speak positive things. Over time, focusing on the positive will allow God to heal your heart and cleanse your mind. After all, the Bible does say that as a man "thinks in his heart, so is he" (Prov. 23:7).

Here are some action steps that I give my coaching clients who have this counterfeit conviction:

1. Make a commitment to be hyperaware of your words and thoughts for a week. Whenever you catch something negative forming in your brain or coming out of your mouth, simply say, "I cancel those words in Jesus' name." You don't have to scream or jump up and down or make a big deal out of it; just say it quietly.

2. Make note of the most common negative things you say, even those things you speak out of self-deprecating humor. After a week, go back and read through your list. Now imagine someone saying those things about someone you care about. How does that make you feel? Well guess what? You're saying those very things about someone God cares very much about, *you*. So knock it off!

3. Ask someone who spends a lot of time with you to call it to your attention whenever you say something negative, especially about your finances. Ask God to help you become more aware of your thoughts. Every time you have a negative thought or say something bad about yourself, continue to pray against those words and thoughts.

4. When negative words and thoughts come, quote a scripture of blessing over yourself. Here's a good one: "God shall supply all your need according to His riches in glory by Christ Jesus" (Phil. 4:19). How can you be poor when your Father in heaven owns it all?

5. Spend some time searching your heart and getting to the root of why you feel poor. Were you poor growing up? Did you lose a business? Did you do some stupid stuff? Understand that who you are in Christ today bears no resemblance to the difficulties and mistakes of the past. Forgive yourself and understand that God already forgave you the moment you asked. Let it go.

Richard Wynn had a successful plumbing business for fifteen years. He did so well that he decided to buy out a friend who had a competing business. The deal looked great on paper, but after the transaction was finalized, Richard starting seeing problems with his friend's business plan. After a couple of months, he figured out that the whole business was a financial house of cards.

Richard spent tens of thousands of dollars trying to clean up the mess and preserve both businesses, but he ended up filing bankruptcy only eighteen months later. Richard, who was a humble and hardworking man, was devastated; he grew up dirt-poor, but bankruptcy? That was something he was sure was making his father turn over in his grave. He took a job working for a nationwide service chain known for offering shoddy work at inflated prices. He started calling himself "Poor Richard," which fit perfectly with his new, self-imposed identity.

My first priority with Richard was to outline the steps that led to the bankruptcy and the businesses' demise. Richard took the failure extra hard because, he said, he really had no one to blame but himself. He had trusted his "friend," but since discovering that his trust was misplaced, Richard felt he could no longer trust his own judgment.

As we talked about the growth of his business and his success prior to taking over his friend's company, Richard admitted that he had always been shocked at his own success, considering his humble beginnings. It became clear that in the back of his mind, failure was always an option for Richard.

We prayed through forgiveness toward the former "friend" and established a time frame for a healthy, biblical confrontation with the friend for a time far, far into the future. And after Richard said he thought he might be suffering from depression since his bankruptcy, I recommended a local psychologist whom he could follow up with for additional help.

But most important, I banished the words "Poor Richard" and replaced them with a play on his name, "Richard wins!" He said he thought it was dorky, and it was, but he promised to try it anyway. And to prove his new mantra wasn't just words, I had Richard make a list of everything he did that made his first business so successful. He also made a list of everything in his life that he was grateful for.

I wasn't sure how grouchy Richard would fare with my goofy mantra and insistence that he focus only on the good. But God filled in the gaps in Richard's heart. He told me later that his gratitude list was so long, he felt kind of silly for beating himself up so much. That improved his outlook enough that he didn't feel the need to follow up with the psychologist.

The words we speak have power, as do the beliefs we hold about ourselves, our potential, and our finances. Money can't change who you are. The only thing that can truly change you is the power of God, and He will change you only if you ask Him to change you. But it doesn't do a whole lot of good to ask God for those changes one minute, then verbally assault yourself, your potential, your intellect, and your future in the next breath. You have to pray for change and back up those prayers with Bible study, obedience to God's Word, and faith in the plans He has for you. And you have to trust in those plans in spite of the appearance of your current circumstances.

> **The words we speak have power.**

That's not necessarily the easiest path for some of us to choose. It takes courage to believe the best when you are walking through the worst. But it's the only way for God to transform your finances, your life, and most important, your heart.

> Dear God, please help me see money the way You see it. And show me that You value me right now for who I am and for who You created me to be. Give me the wisdom and the patience to multiply my resources so that I can be a blessing to others. Let me value my life in terms of the amount of love I give and receive, and not by the number of dollars I have in the bank. Show me what money can do, and just as important, what it cannot do. Help me to find my peace and my safety in You, and only You.
>
> In Jesus' name I pray, amen.

God's Way

Here are the most important points to take away from chapter 2.

- The way we handle money reflects the condition of our hearts.
- It is God's will for His people to live without financial stress and worry.
- Financial problems are never inherently about money, but are instead usually symptoms of underlying spiritual problems.
- Having more or less money doesn't make you more or less of a person. And your bank balance is not reflective of how much God loves you. He loves us all the same.
- We cannot allow fear to undermine our success or stop us from taking risks.
- Being poor for the sake of being poor is no more Christlike than getting rich for the sake of getting rich. We have to strive for balance.
- Greed and the love of money can cause Christians to turn their eyes away from God and start worshipping currency. Therefore, we have to handle with care what God entrusts to us, keeping our wallets open to those in need, and our eyes, minds, and hearts on God.
- Money won't make you happy. Contentment will.
- Even when we think the solution to a problem is money, the solution is always, in fact, more of God.
- Banks go under, stocks crash, and real estate values can plummet. We have to put our trust in God, not in how much money we have at a given time.
- We cannot worship both God and money. We have to choose one.
- Our words have a tremendous amount of power over our lives. What we speak has the power to become what we actually experience.

- When you have a financial setback, be sure you regard it as a temporary circumstance and not a permanent condition.

Solution Steps

Here are simple steps you and your family can take today to help you have a clearer understanding about what money can and cannot do in your life.

1. Jesus told us not to worry, but most of us do plenty of worrying anyway. List the financial concerns you spend the most time worrying about. Then take a moment and pray about each one of those concerns. If you could sit across the table from Jesus right now, what would He say about your worries?

2. In the parable of the talents in Matthew 25, Jesus gave an example of a "wicked and lazy servant" (v. 26) who failed to earn interest on his money out of fear. What areas of your financial life are inhibited by fear? Can you list five things you can do this month to wisely increase the earning capacity of your savings and investments?

3. If someone told you that you had to be poor to be a good Christian, could you list three examples from the Bible to prove that is a counterfeit conviction?

4. Admit it—you've believed at some point in your life that more money would make you happy. List the times in your life that jump to your mind when you believed this. Were you right?

5. In what areas of your financial life are you tempted to put more trust in the numbers on paper and less on God? Can you list examples from your own experience when things didn't go as they were supposed to with your money? How did God provide for you and your family during those times?

6. Find a place in your Bible or in your prayer journal, if you keep one, and write down thoughts on how Proverbs 29:25

is relevant to our current economic crisis. Can this verse help you in times of stress and fear? Explaining your thoughts in your own words will give you a reference point to help you pray through future stresses.

7. Make a list of the last three times you received an unexpected financial windfall, large or small. Was it a pay raise? A tax refund? A gift? An inheritance? Where did the money go? Did the windfall fund any lifestyle upgrades? And did the cost of those upgrades surpass the actual windfall? If you received that same money today, would you make the same choice with it? Why?

8. For one week, be aware of the negative words you speak about yourself, your job, and your finances. Every time you say something negative, pray this out loud: "I cancel those words in Jesus' name."

9. If you notice that you say the same negative things over and over again, ask how you would feel if someone said those things about someone you love. Would you tolerate it?

10. Ask friends and family to call your attention to negative words you speak. The accountability will help you be more aware of the importance of not trash-talking yourself.

11. When negative words or thoughts come, quote a scripture that makes you feel good whenever you hear it or pray.

12. Spend some time searching your heart and your mind and get to the source where those negative thoughts and words are coming from.

THREE

SAVIORS OR ENABLERS?

Let me tell you about the Howards.

Mr. Howard had your typical nine-to-five job, and Mrs. Howard stayed home and cared for little Billy and Janie. Unfortunately, Mr. Howard had a heart attack in his office one day and died at the age of forty-two. Mrs. Howard, only thirty-six herself, was left to care for Billy, seventeen, and Janie, twelve, on her own.

This scenario plays out in thousands of American families every year, and it's no doubt a terrible experience to go through. But the Howards managed to take a sad set of circumstances and turn them into a family legacy that is downright tragic.

Billy got angry about his father's death and joined the Marines, with nary an explanation to his mother and baby sister. One day—poof!—he was gone. Mrs. Howard decided the chain of events—her husband's death and Billy's departure—were somehow all her fault, and she made it her mission to hover over little Janie and protect her from any further damage.

That did not go well.

Darling Janie became a spoiled brat, pretty much overnight. She

44

married right out of high school and divorced a couple of years later, in spite of the thousands of dollars in checks Mrs. Howard wrote to cover the damages every time the couple hit a financial bump.

A little girl was born out of that short union, but darling Janie could not be troubled with raising the child. The baby was left with Mrs. Howard while Janie started the next chapter of her fabulous life, generously funded by her mother.

By now, every dime of Mr. Howard's life insurance proceeds had long since been spent, and Mrs. Howard was working furiously to raise the baby girl, put Janie through graduate school, keep her in designer clothes, and eventually pay for the second wedding, for which Janie dropped out of graduate school a few months before she would have received her master's degree. That marriage didn't last, either.

And it got worse from there.

Janie had yet another couple of failed marriages, bringing the total to four. And all of the weddings and subsequent divorces were paid for by Mrs. Howard, who also managed to make mortgage payments, replace hot water heaters, buy groceries, fund vacations, pay off credit cards, and whatever else was needed to dry little Janie's tears of the moment.

Billy never came around much after the war, but when he did, Mrs. Howard was reduced to an inexplicably guilt-ridden bundle of nerves, hovering and henpecking and doing everything within her power and up to the limit of her credit cards to make his visit "perfect." Billy, however, remained cool and heartless toward his mother and hardly spoke to his sister.

Eventually, Mrs. Howard was forced to file bankruptcy after darling Janie had run up about forty thousand dollars in credit card bills in Mrs. Howard's name and without her knowledge. Mrs. Howard couldn't pay those bills, but she would not have even considered reporting precious Janie to the police for theft. And to make matters worse, not only did Janie never apologize for the fraudulent debt, but she never even acknowledged it. But, then again, Mrs. Howard never asked her to.

It was never spoken of again.

Mrs. Howard died a short time later, and some of her last words were instructions for the granddaughter to always make sure darling Janie was well funded and okay.

Today, Janie is sixty and hasn't worked in ten years. She can't keep a job because no employer will put up with her overwhelming sense of entitlement and her know-it-all attitude. And ironically, Janie blames all the misfortunes of her life on her mother, the long-departed Mrs. Howard, who sacrificed any chance of personal enjoyment or joy in the hopes that by shielding Janie from any inconvenience or responsibility, she would make Janie happy.

And in that pursuit, Mrs. Howard failed. Miserably.

Toxic Assistance

I hope the story of the Howard family gets your attention, because it's quite true, and similar versions of this tale are lived out in families all across America every day. People from all economic and social backgrounds destroy their lives with the thinking that with just one more check, they can "fix" the person they love. They cannot. And because self-sacrifice for the good of others is a Christian value, most of those broken families probably stumble into churches from time to time, if not every Sunday.

> People from all economic and social backgrounds destroy their lives with the thinking that with just one more check, they can "fix" the person they love. They cannot.

Mrs. Howard, for one, never missed a Sunday.

Occasionally her granddaughter would summon the courage to question Mrs. Howard's indulgent behavior toward Janie. Mrs. Howard was quick to respond with a verbal smackdown about helping others, capped off with a quoting of 1 Timothy 5:8, "If anyone does not provide for his own, and especially for those of his household, he has denied the faith and is worse than an unbeliever."

Because that scripture doesn't mince words, it's certainly hard to counter it in an argument about enabling. But what Mrs. Howard and every other well-meaning Christian of her kind fail to do is take it in the context of other biblical teachings, especially examples that we have from the life of Jesus.

Now, to be sure, in biblical times, women who were widowed, abandoned, or divorced by their husbands often returned to their parents. But in those days, women didn't have the right to hold jobs, let alone buy homes and property and otherwise care for themselves in the same way that a man could. A woman was held with no more regard than a head of cattle.

Today, fortunately, women have the same rights as men to make a life for themselves and for their children. And therefore, when able and when necessity arises, they have the responsibility to do so.

Now, you may be wondering, *What constitutes "able?"* How do you determine when someone else is able to take care of him- or herself? Enablers can't ever pinpoint a time when the object of their obsession is able to go it alone. They can't say no.

"Do You Want to Be Made Well?"

An overindulged child becomes an emotionally crippled adult. Let's see how Jesus handled one individual with a more visibly apparent handicap:

After this there was a feast of the Jews, and Jesus went up to Jerusalem. Now there is in Jerusalem by the Sheep Gate a pool, which is called in Hebrew, Bethesda, having five porches. In these lay a great multitude of sick people, blind, lame, paralyzed, waiting for the moving of the water. For an angel went down at a certain time into the pool and stirred up the water; then whoever stepped in first, after the stirring of the water, was made well of whatever disease he had. Now a certain man was there who had an infirmity thirty-eight years. When Jesus saw him lying there, and knew that he already had been in that condition a long time, He said to him, "Do you want to be made well?" The sick man answered Him, "Sir, I have no man to put me into the pool when the water is stirred up; but while I am coming, another steps down before me."

Jesus said to him, "Rise, take up your bed and walk." And immediately the man was made well, took up his bed, and walked. (John 5:1–9)

> An overindulged child becomes an emotionally crippled adult.

This is more than just another great story of one of Jesus' many miracles. This is a classic example of how Jesus dealt with people who were in cycles of harmful behavior.

You may be wondering what I mean by that, when the dude had been so sick for thirty-eight years that he was just lying there. Look at the first thing Jesus said to him. It was a question: "Do you want to be made well?" (v. 6).

Why would Jesus ask that if it wasn't a valid question? We're talking about the Son of God, after all. Jesus had places to go, things to do. He wouldn't waste time on an unnecessary or rhetorical question. He wanted the man to search his heart and see if he truly did want to be well.

But doesn't everyone want to be well?

You would think so, but no. Some people like the attention they get from always being sick or in a state of distress. Some people don't want to take responsibility for their own lives. Others get so comfortable sitting for so long by the side of the pool that the thought of life somewhere else, even a healthier place, becomes scary. And sometimes people get addicted to being rescued.

So they sit there and complain.

Look at the man's response to Jesus' question: "Sir, I have no man to put me into the pool when the water is stirred up; but while I am coming, another steps down before me" (v. 7).

Whine, whine, whine.

After so many failures, couldn't the man figure out a way to sit there with his feet at the edge of the water so when the angel came around, he could be the first in? The phrase "while I am coming" indicates that he definitely had some mobility—he wasn't completely helpless—yet he blamed his state on not having someone else "to put me into the pool."

The passage says the angel went down "at a certain time" (v. 4). After so many occurrences, wouldn't that timing and that pattern have become very apparent to a man who should have had healing at the top of his list of things to do?

Yet many emotionally crippled people fail to recognize the patterns that keep them in the same state.

> **Many emotionally crippled people fail to recognize the patterns that keep them in the same state.**

The House of Grace

The sick man was trying to get into the pool of Bethesda. In Hebrew, the name Bethesda means, "Place of outpouring," or "House of grace." I love that. To Jesus, extending true grace and healing meant confronting the sick man's reluctance to go after his healing. Unfortunately, too many Christians today don't equate outpouring and grace with asking difficult, pointed questions and administering tough love. And it's a shame.

You can bet every time a water heater died, a transmission went out, or a light bill needed to be paid, Janie Howard was armed with a long list of reasons why she had to go running to her momma instead of handling the problem herself or with her husband of the moment. And the result was not that one day Mrs. Howard finally met the last need and Janie was "okay." It meant that the sum of all of Mrs.

Howard's efforts resulted in a grown woman who remains incapable of taking care of herself. She's crippled in the worst possible way.

"Do you want to be made well?" This is a question for all of us. It's a question you need to ask of the people you strive to assist, be they family members, friends, or even strangers. Even when someone tells you that, yes, he wants to be healed, you have to exercise discernment. Someone can say, "Yes! I want to be well!" while her actions indicate that the answer is, in fact, no.

Drug addicts often want help, and they always need money. It's the same thing with chronic alcoholics, pornography addicts, and people with spending problems. What kind of help do they want? If they are still unhealthy, they want your money. What kind of help do they need? What they need is a firm no, and medical or psychological help when warranted. They need tough love.

Life-Endangering Enabling

Georgiana had once been a beautiful brunette with bright blue eyes, gorgeous ivory skin, and a radiant smile, but not on the day she came into my office.

As she sat in one of my office chairs, she was visibly weaving around like a drunk person, looking as if she could fall over onto the floor with the slightest breeze. Her eyes were glassy and unfocused. Her hair was a ratted mess, and her skin was mottled and dull. She rambled on so fast I could hardly understand her. But she repeated over and over again different dollar amounts that she wanted—now.

"I need five hundred dollars! I need it now. I'm a tithing member of this church, and you have to help me!" Before I could even answer, she blurted out, "What about four hundred? Could you do four hundred? Three hundred? You have got to help me!"

When I asked her what she needed money for, she reached into her bag and handed me a fistful of prescriptions for various painkillers, anxiety medications, and other drugs.

Georgiana was high as a kite and wanted more.

Her husband had left her the year before, and she coped with the pain of her loss by taking lots and lots of pills. And now she was hooked.

I tried to start a conversation about rehab, but she angrily snatched up her prescriptions and her purse and staggered out of my office before I could finish getting the words out. She was so out of it that if she hadn't already told me a friend had driven her to the church, I would have tackled her to get her car keys.

I was thrilled when her sister called me the next day. Initially I thought, *Great! Her family is aware of her addiction, and now we can work together to get her the help she needs.* How wrong I was.

Her sister acknowledged that Georgiana had a serious and life-threatening drug addiction and even volunteered that everyone in the family had helped her all they could and had had enough of her behavior. Yet she insisted I give her money for more pills and irately refused to discuss Georgiana's need to go into drug rehab.

I found out later that a group of people at the church who knew and loved Georgiana tried to help by working to convince her to go into drug rehab. But in response, Georgiana threw her friends out of her house.

Soon after, Georgiana disappeared. I hope she got some help, but I am left to wonder, because she severed all ties with her church after her friends' intervention.

The Difficulty of Saying No

While the Bible doesn't deal with enabling directly, Jesus gives us good insight on dealing with difficult people. Can you imagine Him giving a drunk man money to buy more booze? Or paying off the credit cards of someone who cannot stop her out-of-control and unnecessary spending? Or buying pills for a drug addict? What about paying rent for months on end for an able-bodied person who refuses to get a job? Well, of course we can't imagine Jesus doing any of those things. So why do "well-meaning" Christians do them every day?

Counterfeit convictions.

> **Most well-meaning believers have a hard time discerning the difference between meeting a need and filling someone else's personal void.**

As Christians, it's important for us to feel as though we are doing good things that help other people. However, most well-meaning believers have a hard time discerning the difference between meeting a need and filling someone else's personal void. And we wrongly think that it must be a sin to say no. And in my experience, saying no to a controlling, manipulative person does not yield pleasant results. He or she will accuse you of lacking compassion, not caring, and will question your very salvation, all in the name of getting you to cough up assistance just one more time. Say no.

Counterfeit Conviction: It is my Christian duty to be at the beck and call of everyone who wants me to help them out of a jam.

Timeless Truth: You have to take care of yourself if you're going to be in a position to help anyone else. And the world is full of people who live to take advantage of generous souls. Generosity and a desire to be helpful to others must be coupled with wisdom and discernment.

Proverbs 1:32 says, "The complacency of fools will destroy them." In my office, I apply that scripture like this: "I'm not going to work harder on your problem than you are." And if this is the fifth, sixth, or even seventh time you've found yourself sailing in the same uncomfortable boat, your solution lies not in assistance from someone else but in a reckoning with what's going on between your ears and in your heart.

I'll certainly help you, but I would venture to guess the kind of help I'm going to offer is not going to be the kind of help you're asking for.

Disabling the Enablers

I might pick on indulgent parents, I know: the wretched plight of the Super Dad, Super Mom, and heaven help us, Super Parents. Never to be outdone is the Super Grandma. Always there to save the day with a mighty stroke of the pen to the checkbook.

But it's not just family members who enable bad or destructive behavior. I've met the Super Landlord, the Super Boss, and many other well-meaning people who could leap over healthy social parameters in a single bound. In reality, though, my friend, that *S* on your chest doesn't stand for "Super." It stands for "Sucker." If you continue bailing someone out, especially if it is to your own personal financial peril, you're not a savior; you're an enabler. The key word here is "continue." Sacrificial giving, when warranted, is a tremendous blessing for both parties. Continually bailing someone out who refuses to get his or her life in order is a blessing for no one.

> **If you continue bailing someone out, especially if it is to your own personal financial peril, you're not a savior; you're an enabler.**

Most of us have enabled someone else's bad behavior at one time or another. But a few folks take it to a whole other level and could give the federal government a run for its money when it comes to bailouts. How do you know when you've crossed the line? There is a common pattern of deceptive feelings that accompany trying to be a "super" anything. When someone repeatedly bails out others to his own detriment, and then makes up justifications for doing so, though his "help" becomes a hindrance, the truth is, for a serial enabler, the behavior feels *good*.

Some of the fuzzy feelings of enabling:

It makes us feel needed.

Everybody wants to feel needed. We have a deep, human desire to feel connected to others in a unique way. Mothers love to feel needed by their children. Friends need to know that those in their circle seek their companionship.

But in keeping a loved one tied to your apron strings, so to speak, or to keep her needing you by bailing her out financially or allowing her bad behavior, you are creating a need based on wounds and lies that will only grow deeper and more toxic with time.

It makes us feel powerful and important.

Saving someone else's day is a powerful thing. Being *the* person someone else has to run to can be quite a power trip. But it's a very unhealthy kind of power, for you and for your "dependent." Think of it this way: is the person you're "helping" calling on you more often than he or she calls on God?

Janie Howard, for one, has a nonexistent prayer life and a terrible relationship with God. Why? Because her whole life, she called on momma, not God, when she needed something. At this point, she probably has no idea how to call on God, and she doesn't have much hope in learning how because she won't go to church.

Sometimes a speedy response is the worst thing in the world for a chronically needy person. Here's a truth for all of us: We've got to get on our knees and pray to God *before* we reach out to others, or before we give to those reaching out to us. *It's the right thing to do.*

Helping others comes naturally to people who want to be more like Jesus. What we need to carefully analyze is whether the assistance we're contemplating is actually going to *help* the situation. Here are some questions to ask before you jump on your white horse:

1. Has this person asked for this kind of help from you before?
2. Is it something he can eventually work out on his own?
3. Is this circumstance due to an addiction or other destructive behavior?
4. Have other people already had it with this individual and washed their hands of the situation?
5. Have you ever uttered the words, "If he would only ____" in regard to this person?

6. Is the problem due to circumstances within this individual's control?

If you answered "yes" to three or more of these questions, you may seriously want to consider withholding your assistance.

For example, if your brother loses his job, you may want to help him with some extra cash. But if he's lost his sixth job in four months, you may not want to contribute toward his video game addiction.

And if other people in a dependent person's inner circle have washed their hands of the recurring drama, you might want to ask yourself if you really want to be next in line for certain failure.

The hardest question to honestly evaluate is whether the person has control over his or her circumstances. This takes a healthy dose of clear thinking and maturity. Hypochondria does not excuse a person from gainful employment. Neither does depression excuse excessive drinking or drug use. And having a rotten set of circumstances does not give someone permission to treat others like a doormat. There are healthy ways to deal with setbacks. Help a hurting person find them.

> **There are healthy ways to deal with setbacks.**

It makes us feel less pressured because it's the path of least resistance.

Saying no is hard. Sticking to it is harder. Saying no over and over to someone who is used to pushing others around can become a part-time job. Stick to your guns. You'll be glad you did—and eventually, so will the individual who leans on you.

It makes us feel fulfilled because it has become a habit.

We all have habits. Some are situational, like turning on the TV while we cook dinner, calling our best friend while we fold laundry, or eating Nacho Cheese Doritos when football's on. Others are behavioral, like nail biting, doodling, hair twirling. The ones you really have to watch out for are the reactionary ones, like reaching for your checkbook as soon as you see your sister's name on the caller ID.

Don't say yes just because you *always* say yes. Perhaps it is time to say no.

It's all up to you.

This is seriously dangerous territory. Manipulative people love to tell their enablers that they are their only hope for survival. I've had otherwise rational adults bawling like toddlers in my office because an adult child of theirs has threatened suicide if the parents don't pay off the brat's maxed-out credit cards once again.

What?

Children—and sometimes even grown children—are like gamblers. They only pull that lever on the slot machine because they know eventually there's going to be a payout.

I've also counseled parents whose "kids" have threatened to cut off all communication and withhold contact from grandchildren if the parents don't pay up on a list of demands. This is ridiculous. It's emotional extortion, and it happens every day in families that look perfectly healthy from the outside.

Call their bluff. I mean it. Now, I don't mean to double-dog dare someone to commit suicide, but when the conversation heads toward threats, walk away. Hang up the phone. Refuse to participate. Don't listen. You can't be a pawn in someone's sick little game if you're not willing to step on the chessboard. You may not see your grandkids for a week or two, but eventually, if you put your foot down, your children will relent. And as an added bonus, they may actually come to *respect* you.

> You can't be a pawn in someone's sick little game if you're not willing to step on the chessboard.

Excuses, Excuses

One of the more extreme and expensive cases of parental enabling came from David and Jan Stewart. David and Jan had $150,000 in debt, not including the mortgage on their home. Every dime of the debt was in student loans they had taken out on behalf of their four sons. And that wasn't the worst of it: they had cashed out all their retirement savings on top of taking out loans to provide the top-tier private college educations they thought their little darlings were entitled to. And *that* wasn't the worst of it: Three of their sons had dropped out of college without even getting degrees, and all four kids were unemployed and still living at home.

And even *that* wasn't the worst of it. Only two years prior, David had made a cool $500,000 from the sale of a business, and every dime of that money was *gone*.

They were spending $1,200 a month to feed their "little" darlings and wanting to know how to avoid falling behind on the student loan payments, which, by that point, dwarfed their mortgage payment. When I suggested they demand that those four grown men get jobs to help out with the household expenses, David's reply was, "Oh, we could never do that."

It's easy to shake our heads in disbelief at such blatant and reckless enabling, but I would venture to guess that on any given day, thousands of pastors are having counseling sessions in their offices with families dealing with similar, if less egregious, circumstances. I could tell story after story after story with similar circumstances, but they all have the same ending: bailouts help no one.

If in reading this chapter you recognize that you are enabling someone else's destructive behavior, I hope you've found the courage to recognize that your situation is not any different. It may not be as appalling as David and Jan's, but it won't have a happier ending unless you find the strength to let go and let the person figure it out for himself. Only by allowing someone you love to stand on his own two feet are you truly helping him. Here are some strategies to help you reset your pattern:

1. Make a list detailing every time you have come to his rescue. Ask others to help you recall different events, as your memory may be a little selective at this point. At the end

of each entry, briefly list whether the assistance really was a catalyst for meaningful and permanent change. "Johnny's lights were not turned off because I paid the bill" is not to be considered success if you've paid the bill more than once in the last twenty-four months.

2. List the actual consequences of your staying out of the situation. Is it really the end of the world if Johnny sits in the dark for a couple of days? No, it is not.

   Usually, parents of adults acting like children look at me as though I'm Satan in a red wig when I suggest they allow their little darling's electricity to be shut off: as if death is imminent if ESPN won't come on. "But it's cold outside!" one mother of a deadbeat son wailed to me. This particular woman had paid her son's light bill five out of the last six months.

   "It's fifty degrees!" I said. "I'm sure he has a sweater."

   I thought she was going to pass out.

   I received no commitment from that mom that day to stop shelling out checks for electric bills, but she did call me about eight months later with some news: "I was really shocked that you would tell me not to pay his bill," she said. "And it took a couple more months of check writing for me to wonder what would happen if I didn't pay it. Finally I got so fed up, I refused to pay. He wouldn't pay it, so his electricity was turned off. He was so mad at me! But you know, he got over it. He paid the bill, and he hasn't asked me for anything since."

   Victory!

3. List the ways your "assistance" has allowed the person to continue bad behavior. By paying the electric bill, did you free up money in Johnny's budget for booze? Be honest. Truthfully evaluate whether your assistance is helping the person you're enabling—or keeping him stuck in a cycle of dependence.

4. Establish a budget in which your tithe and your most immediate needs (food, clothing, shelter, transportation) are covered

first, followed by your secondary goals and obligations (retirement savings, debt elimination, mortgage payoff acceleration, vacation savings). You cannot give away money that you do not have.

5. Set aside a monthly amount to use for "spontaneous" giving or helping others. If after making your budget you don't have money left over, then you are about to get a crash course in saying no.

When Saying No Is the Way to Help

Super Landlords Martin and Teresa Garcia were about to go into foreclosure on a rental property they owned and had even fallen behind on their own house payments in an effort to keep from losing the rental property. Counting the mortgage payments that were past due, they were close to $200,000 in debt, not counting the principal balances on their mortgages. They came to see me for guidance and revealed that the tenants had not paid rent in *ten months*.

"And why," I asked, "have you not evicted them?" The thought hadn't occurred to them. Their tenants were really nice people, and Christians, too, they argued. Surely they were going to get their finances in order any day now and start paying rent. "We can't evict them!" Teresa argued. "That just doesn't seem like the Christian thing to do!"

First I asked them if they were in a financial position to provide free housing to a couple they barely knew. Their quick answer was no.

Next we ran their numbers together and saw that they were three months, at most, from dual foreclosures and bankruptcy. That finally made the lights come on in their heads, alerting them that they had to take action swiftly. There was no time to lose.

We wrote down an action plan, which they followed to the letter:

1. They called the couple right away and set a time to meet face-to-face the very next day. At the meeting, Martin and Teresa kindly but firmly gave their tenants an unchangeable

four-week deadline to catch up on the back rent or face eviction.

2. They prayed with the other couple but did not apologize for putting their foot down. They refused to engage in any discussion of the circumstances of the tenants' financial distress, and they kept the conversation focused on the back rent and eminent eviction.

3. They got the tenants to sign a letter acknowledging the requirements to stay in the home. That eliminated the chance of future arguments or "confusion" about what was expected.

And the result? Within a month, the tenants paid back a healthy portion of the past-due rent. Those same tenants also dealt with their own financial mess, and they realized they were overextended on the rental. They moved out peacefully, allowing Martin and Teresa to put the home up for sale.

The home sold right away in a pitiful market, which demonstrated to all of us the awesome power and mercy that God shows us when we finally decide to step up and do the right thing. The Garcias even made some money off the sale, which enabled them to catch up on their primary home mortgage and pay off additional debt. Within six months they had paid off the rest of their credit cards and had begun working on their retirement savings once again.

Please understand that while saying no to someone who is trapped in a cycle of bad decisions and habits may be hard, it is the very best thing you can do to help that person. You'll have better control over your own finances and your "no" may finally be the thing that encourages her to grow up and stand on her own two feet. Continuing to be an enabler will have tragic consequences not only for you, but also for the person you are trying to help. By continuing to step in to be someone's "savior," you not only block that person from becoming independent, but you're also keeping him or her from seeking the help that comes from the only one true savior, Jesus Christ.

Think about it this way: spiritually weak people only pray about their needs. If you're meeting the needs, why should they pray? Is there any chance, any chance at all, that God is going to bless these circumstances?

> **Insurmountable circumstances are one thing; bottomless excuses are another.**

Again, please don't confuse the message of this chapter with a call to refuse aid to legitimately hurting people facing unusual and insurmountable circumstances. They do arise. And as Christians, we should certainly help. But those types of situations don't occur again and again and again in an increasingly mundane format with the same person. Insurmountable circumstances are one thing; bottomless excuses are another. Know the difference. Have courage. Help when warranted, but otherwise, close your checkbook and say no.

A prayer for enablers:

Dear God, I lift up to You this person I have been trying to help. I acknowledge that I have been trying to be [his/her] savior, when in fact, only You can truly save [him/her]. Lord, please give me patience, wisdom, and the courage to say no when I need to. Help me to see when my actions are hindering someone rather than helping him or her. Help me lead others to You as the source of anything they could possibly need. Help me to care for myself and those who are truly dependent on me first, and help me set financial priorities that honor You. Remove from me, God, any feelings of guilt for saying no when it's the right thing to do. Give me peace, Lord, and bless this other person as You fill [him/her] with peace as well.

In Jesus' name I pray, amen.

God's Way

Here are the most important points to take away from chapter 3.

- It is impossible to fix someone else's life. A person has to fix it for himself or herself.
- An overindulged child who becomes an overindulged adult is crippled emotionally.
- Some people like the attention they get from always being sick or in a state of distress, and some people don't want to take responsibility for their own lives.
- Emotionally crippled people fail to recognize the patterns that keep them in the same state.
- Throughout the New Testament, Jesus gives us good examples on how to deal with difficult people.
- It is important to discern whether you are meeting someone's need or filling a personal void.
- You have to take care of yourself if you're going to be in a position to help anyone else—and the world is full of people who live to take advantage of generous souls. Generosity and a desire to be helpful to others must be coupled with wisdom and discernment.
- Never work harder on someone else's problem than he or she is working.
- If you continue bailing someone else out, especially if it is to your own personal financial peril, you're not a savior— you're an enabler.
- Sometimes a speedy response is the worst thing in the world for a chronically needy person.
- We have to truthfully evaluate whether our assistance is helping someone or keeping that individual stuck in a cycle of dependence.

Solution Steps

Here are simple steps you and your family can take today to help you know when to help someone and when to let that person stand on his or her own two feet.

1. Have there been setbacks in your family that led to enabling? List two or three examples, and then list behaviors that might have been more beneficial in the long run.
2. Answer the following questions: Have you ever tried to "fix" someone with a check? How did it work out?
3. Is someone in your life constantly draining your time, energy, and resources, yet he or she never seems to get any better? Set up a convenient time for a talk with this person. Before you meet, list all the times you have helped him or her, and the result. Use specific examples. When you meet, be kind but firm, and establish boundaries for the relationship and for future help.
4. When you have a needy person in your life, consider using an algebraic method of setting boundaries: $X + Y = Z$. For example, if your adult daughter has overdrawn her checkbook again, and is asking for you to cover the charges—again—you could say, "If you will attend a budgeting class [X], and if you will start using cash envelopes to manage your money better [Y], then [=] I will help you one more time [Z]. Do it again, though, and you're on your own."
5. In your prayer journal or in your Bible, list some things that will help you discern whether someone is truly in need or just wanting you to fix a problem.
6. Read the story of the lame man at the pool of Bethesda. Jesus asked the man, "Do you want to be made well?" What sources of pain do you most often see people hanging on to? Can you think of ways you might be able to help them seek God's healing? For example, if most of your friends are

caught in a cycle of overspending and debt because they don't
want to face the difficulty of changing their ways, could you
offer to coach them on money management or attend a budgeting class with them?

7. Take a few moments and ponder the phrase "tough love."
Does it have a positive or a negative connotation to you?
If you're married, how does your spouse feel about this
phrase? If you have different opinions, is this a source of
conflict in your marriage? Discuss with your spouse ways
you can come to agreement about when to help others out
and when to say no.

8. When someone asks for your help, ask the following questions before you whip out your checkbook:

- Has this ever happened before?
- Is this something he can eventually work out on his own?
- Is this circumstance due to an addiction or other destruc-
  tive behavior?
- Have other people already had it with him?
- Have I ever said, "If he would only _____" in regard to
  this person?
- Is the problem due to circumstances within his control?

If the answer to three or more of these questions is yes, your
answer probably needs to be no.

9. If you're an enabler, here are strategies to help you reset your
pattern:

- Make a list detailing every time you have come to this
  person's rescue. Ask others to help you recall different
  events, as your memory may be a little selective at this
  point. At the end of each entry, briefly list whether the
  assistance really was a catalyst for meaningful and permanent change.

- List the *actual* consequences of your staying out of the situation.
- List the ways your "assistance" has allowed the person to continue bad behavior. Truthfully evaluate whether your assistance is helping that person or keeping him or her stuck in a cycle of dependence.
- Establish a budget in which your tithe and your most immediate needs (food, clothing, shelter, transportation) are covered first, followed by your secondary goals and obligations (retirement savings, debt elimination, mortgage payoff acceleration, vacation savings). You cannot give away money that you do not have.
- Set aside a monthly amount to use for "spontaneous" giving or helping others. If after making your budget you don't have money left over, then you are about to get a crash course in saying no.

FOUR

SELF-RIGHTEOUS SLACKERS

Charlie and Erica had it all: a brand-new home in a nice neighborhood, two new cars, and a month-old baby boy.

They also had lots of debt to go with their American dream. Both cars were financed, and the combined payments were 25 percent of Charlie's take-home pay. The payments on the lovely home took up another 50 percent of Charlie's pay. And while they boasted of having no credit card debt—"We're not stupid!" Erica explained—they had another $200,000 in student loan debt for Erica's education, a master's degree in education from a well-known Christian university.

With the house, the cars, and Erica's student loans, the couple was $532,000 in debt and they had not even celebrated their first anniversary. Yikes.

Charlie was proud of his $75,000 starting salary as an IT support guy for a local communications company, as well he should have been. The job market was tough, but Charlie was smart and tenacious, and he found a good job quickly, right out of school.

They were so happy about Charlie's great new job that they bought a $275,000 home, a pretty luxurious choice considering it was 30 percent higher than the median home price in their area.

Erica was so freshly graduated from college that the ink wasn't even dry on her diploma, so I asked her how her job search was going and what the school districts in our area were paying for a first-year teacher with a master's degree.

"Oh no," she said, glancing down at her sleeping baby. "I'm not going to work. God told me years ago to stay home once I became a mother. It happened much sooner than we planned, but I have to do what's right for our son. I don't believe in day care. I won't have strangers raising my baby!"

Her voice got higher and shriller as she spoke, and by the time she finished her little speech, Erica was positively shouting at me. And I had only inquired about her job search, a reasonable question for a recent college graduate with as much education debt as some newly minted doctors.

"But Erica, your education debt is almost as much as your mortgage," I said. "You two can't make ends meet as it is. What are you going to do when you have to start making payments on those student loans? Where is that money going to come from?"

Her answer made my head hurt.

"That's why we're here. We were hoping you could tell us," she said.

More than half a million dollars in the hole, and they're expecting someone else to fix it.

Erica had been out of school a month, which meant she had five months to go before loan payments started. I started thinking of what possibilities they might have. Their savings was negligible. They were just starting out, so they had nothing of value to sell to raise cash. The house was mortgaged to the hilt, and they were upside down on both cars, meaning they owed more on the loans than the cars were worth. Ruling out a lottery win or a sudden inheritance from a rich uncle (they had none—I checked), this sweet young family was bound for ruin before they even really got off the ground.

They did have one thing working in their favor, though: both of their mothers were retired, and both lived in town. Jackpot.

"Erica, are you close to your mom? Is she excited about the baby?" I asked.

"Oh yes!" she said. "My mom is my best friend, and she's over the moon that she gets to be a grandma now. She's over at our house pretty much every day."

And from Charlie's description, his mom seemed to be just as involved in the couple's life as Erica's. We were starting to get somewhere.

While it was pointless to lecture them on the stupidity of student loans, especially such an insane amount for a degree in a field not known for high pay, I thought I might invoke a little old-fashioned guilt on Erica. Even though I already knew the answer, I asked: "Erica, how much of these loans are yours and how much are Charlie's?"

"They're all mine," she said.

"And Charlie," I continued, "you have a master's degree as well, right? Did you graduate with any student loan debt?"

"No I didn't," he replied. "I worked two, sometimes three jobs the entire time I was in school, but I got out debt free."

"That's great, Charlie," I said. Then turning to Erica, I put the hammer down. "Erica, did you pay for any of your schooling while you were taking classes?" I asked.

"No," she said, her eyes averted as she suddenly became very interested in the baby, whose carrier was on the floor at her feet. "I mean, I was busy. I was in a sorority, and those take a lot of time. And I was in the choir, and my friends from my dorm always had me doing something with them."

In short, she was a party girl. A good little Christian party girl, but a party girl nonetheless. Not only that, but because her family was of limited means, she was responsible for all of her expenses in college, and all were financed through loans: meals, books, dorm fees, car insurance, gasoline, dinners out with friends, new clothes, medical expenses. You name it; she had gone into hock for it.

Neither Charlie's nor Erica's parents could afford to put them through college. But that's normal: most of us don't get a free ride. What I wanted to drive home to them was that even though they had similar situations, and both had gone to expensive private schools and gotten master's degrees, they got them in very different ways and with very different levels of maturity.

The bottom line was that Erica had a grand old time in college, which was essentially an extension of her high school years. And now she planned to have a grand old time in adulthood, letting someone else—poor, patient Charlie—worry about the massive debt she'd racked up in school. And Charlie, sweet and quiet as he was, appeared ready to let his spoiled wife do just that.

"What about forbearance? Or deferment? A couple of my friends have done those, and they didn't have to make payments," Erica said.

"You could check and see if you qualified for deferment, but all that does is delay your payments for a few months. You're just putting off the inevitable. Plus, you would have to apply individually to all of your different lenders, and each lender likely has different rules for qualifications for deferment. And they may not all agree," I said. At last count, Erica had loans with thirteen different companies. Ouch.

The main reason deferment was a terrible idea for Erica was that if it were awarded to her, she might never consider going back to work. Plus, deferment is a big deal. Even if she were approved, she might never be able to get it again, and she might need that option even more at a later time—if she or the baby were to become sick, for example. The only reason she had right now for not earning money to make payments was that she didn't want to.

"And forbearance is a terrible idea," I continued. "Interest will continue to accumulate, and your loan balance will just keep getting bigger."

Erica had a comeback for that too.

"Well, the type of work that Charlie does is really in demand. He has already been offered consulting jobs on the side," she said. "He can just do that for a while until the loans are paid."

Now Charlie was the one looking at the floor. He didn't say a word. My heart broke a little for him, and I could see his brain ticking through thoughts of another four to six years of sixteen-hour days, just as he had done in college.

"Erica, this is the first time in his adult life that Charlie has had only one job. Think about what you are asking him to do," I said. "This is his baby, too, and I'm sure Charlie would like to spend some time with his son and his new wife rather than spend the next few years paying off your loans. Do you really think this plan of yours is fair?"

Red faced and sputtering, she stood up and picked up the baby carrier and the diaper bag. "This is ridiculous! I didn't come here for this! You can't tell me I have to work when God told me to stay home with my baby!" she shouted. "Charlie, we're leaving!"

Charlie's reaction was even more shocking.

"No, we're not," he said, calmly. "Sit down. We are going to figure out a plan. You are acting like a child. And your tantrums are what got us into this mess. You went to your mother's for three days when I tried to talk you into buying a less expensive house. And you demanded we buy those cars because your friends had new cars, even though we didn't need them. I've had enough. Sit down and listen, and let's work out a plan."

Whoa, Nellie! I don't know whose jaw hit the floor first—mine or Erica's—but she sat down, straightened her shoulders, and looked me in the eye for the first time in ten minutes.

"Erica, I know how you feel about staying home with your baby. I really do. It's a wonderful goal to have," I said. "But by racking up all that debt in college, you eliminated being a stay-at-home mom as a viable choice for you for your first years out of college. The Bible tells us that it is wicked to borrow and not repay. [See Psalm 37:21.] You cannot get out of the obligation that you created for yourself, and you can't just hoist it all on Charlie's shoulders or demand that I find a way to fix it. This is your problem, and you are going to have to work to fix it."

Erica started to cry. But I think that while we all realized she had walked into my office a petulant child, she was leaving a responsible woman. We had just tackled a core issue that would have caused financial sabotage, potentially for the rest of her life.

Her problem was that while she had plans for her life based on values she wanted to uphold, such as being a stay-at-home mom, her actions were in direct conflict with her values. When the baby came, she intended to keep her plans to be a stay-at-home mom, refusing to acknowledge that she had essentially made another choice—to rack up tons of student loan debt—which trumped her original choice.

It's like playing a game of draw poker: once you put some of your cards down on the table and get new ones, you can't play the game based on the original hand you drew. You have to play the game with the cards that are in your hand at that moment. And refusing to acknowledge that the game has changed is childish and will lead to financial sabotage every time.

> Refusing to acknowledge that the game has changed is childish and will lead to financial sabotage every time.

But when the original plans line up with godly goals, it can be really hard to acknowledge that you can't do what you intended. That was Erica's problem. Her Christian ideal was to stay home with her baby. However, she traded her choice for the enjoyment of a work-free college life, paid for with student loans.

Counterfeit Conviction: God didn't tell me to go to work. My economic success is up to God, and I don't have anything to do with it. I have a good reason not to go to work, so I won't. My responsibilities will be met somehow.

Timeless Truth: Laziness does not honor God; neither is it His plan for your life. However, God always blesses hard work and dedication.

"If anyone will not work, neither shall he eat," is the warning of 2 Thessalonians 3:10. And Psalm 37:21 says, "The wicked borrows and does not repay." Pretty simple. If you have obligations, and worse, if you have debt, God won't tell you it's okay not to work unless He has provided a means for you to meet those obligations and to pay your debts beforehand.

Here's an even more direct example: the Ten Commandments. And while "Thou shalt work for a living" is not one of them, it is certainly implied. The fourth commandment, "Remember the Sabbath, to keep it holy," is found in Exodus 20:8. But read on to verse 9 and you'll find this: "Six days you shall labor and do all your work." So if you're waiting for the voice of God to tell you to get a job, pop in that Charlton Heston movie if you need to, but I don't think it gets any clearer than this.

But if you would like one more example, consider Proverbs 24:33–34, which reads, "A little sleep, a little slumber, a little folding of the hands to rest; so shall your poverty come like a prowler, and your need like an armed man."

A Little Hope

To encourage Erica, I showed her that even after taxes, work clothing, and other incidental expenses, if she could earn her projected salary of $50,000 a year as a high school advanced-placement math teacher, she could knock out her debt in about five years or so. Plus, she would have the joy and personal satisfaction of not only getting some use out of her very expensive education, but also from spending time in the field she was obviously passionate about.

She wasn't happy, but she listened, and they left with her promising to fully explore her options. Three weeks later she called me with an update, and she was so excited that I could hardly recognize her voice.

She explained that she had landed a spot at her neighborhood high school, and the principal was so happy with Erica's credentials that she gladly gave Erica the okay to go home for lunch and leave the campus immediately after her last class ended at 2:30. With Erica's two-minute commute to work, she could get up at 5 a.m. and have two hours with the baby before starting her workday at 7 a.m.

The two grandmothers worked out a schedule where one came over Mondays, Wednesdays, and Fridays, and the other came Tuesdays and Thursdays. They would put the baby down for his first nap after Erica left for work and have him up when she came home for lunch. Then the baby could have his afternoon nap and be up when she came home from school.

"All I will be missing is naptimes!" she said. "I can do this!"

What's more, one of their neighbors was so enamored with Erica's new car that she was able to sell it to him for what she owed on it. Erica's dad gave her his old Subaru, which she was glad to have in lieu of the car payment.

"And Charlie is so relieved. He's so much happier and more relaxed now," she said. "And he's really proud of me. He really respects the choice I made."

Charlie and Erica still had a gargantuan mess to dig out of, but at least they had a plan now, and the numbers showed in black and white that it was possible for them to be debt free much more quickly than they ever imagined. And more important, Erica learned to grow up and take responsibility for her decisions, and Charlie learned how to stand up and say no to his new wife when she was being impractical. He also experienced the mystery of marriage by being the tool of God's correction. That's what you sign up for, people.

Opting Out of the Office

I like Charlie and Erica's story because it highlights that student loans are, in my opinion, one of the closest things we have to hell on earth, and it also showcases to a fine degree the group of people who fight the hardest not to get a job: moms. I think being a stay-at-home mom is a fantastic privilege, but it is just that: a privilege. It is *not* a right. You can either afford it or you can't, and the numbers don't lie.

The truth is, most American families spend every dime of their two incomes, and then some. And most aren't willing to make the necessary sacrifices for mom—or dad—to stay home with the children.

If you've planned wisely and made those sacrifices to stay home with your children, my hat is off to you. But if you've spent money as if your name is P. Diddy, and you live beyond your means, please don't trot around on your high horse, saying God told you not to work. If

> **Most American families spend every dime of their two incomes, and then some.**

you really feel that you have a mandate from God to stay home while your children are young, then you sure better live and save accordingly or you will have an Erica-sized mess on your hands.

However, if you have lived and spent like a rap star, well, welcome to the real world. You better work out a plan that is the very best it can be for your children, and get thyself a paycheck. Work hard, be smart, and maybe you can minimize the amount of time you need to be away from your family.

And before some of you ladies come after me with torches and pitchforks, let me note that I am the mother of three rambunctious little boys. After my oldest was born, and again after my twins were born, I had the siren call in my heart to stay home and be with them 24-7. But the first time, my grandmother lived with us, and I was blessed with a flexible schedule at the newspaper, which was a whopping five-minute drive from my house. Like Erica, I was only missing naptimes, and frankly, it would have been stupid to quit a job I loved that allowed so much flexibility combined with a good income.

Before the twins were born, I had racked up a ton of credit card debt. I accomplished this feat by running through Neiman Marcus with my credit cards, figuring this would somehow mitigate my fear of having two babies at once. Then my grief over the death of my grandmother, who passed away when the twins were only six weeks old, compounded the problem. So at that time, staying home wasn't a choice.

Besides, we had found a wonderful Christian woman to watch the kids in our home, and while her salary was more than our mortgage payment, we knew it was a temporary sacrifice. On the other hand, chucking my career would have permanent financial consequences. I had flexible hours, great pay, and a boatload of debt to pay off. I needed to stay, so I did.

What really breaks my heart is when a stay-at-home mom finds herself newly single because her husband died or left her, or because she left because of abuse or infidelity. While I bring the hammer down on lazy couch potatoes who don't want to put their noses to the grindstone, I have a lot more compassion for women whose lives have taken a harsh turn through no fault of their own. It must be hard to wrap your brain around the reality that you now have to leave your little darlings in someone else's care so that you can go make a living to support them. But if you're on your own, this is a reality you must face. Go talk to your pastor or some of the leaders in your church and surround yourself with support as you make this dramatic life change. It won't be easy, but *God has promised that* He will "never leave you nor forsake you" (Heb. 13:5). He will walk alongside you and your children as you navigate this new path.

> God has promised that He will "never leave you nor forsake you."

It may not be the life you envisioned for yourself, but it will be okay. I promise. And God will certainly bless your efforts to support yourself and your children.

The Next Big Thing

As much as I've picked on moms here, at least I can say their desire not to work is a valid one. I can't give the same latitude to most of the men and their reasons for not working.

My all-time favorite professional loafer is a guy named Andrew Pepperdine. Andrew was smart, a smooth talker, and he had the persistence of a used-car salesman.

Andrew didn't attend our church, but I guess he drove by and saw our big building and figured we must have deep pockets and empty brains. He wanted $3,000, right now, thank you very much, to pay his rent and the payments on his two cars.

Now, Andrew was no ordinary man (or so he thought), and he sure wasn't going to drive any ordinary cars. Andrew drove a Mercedes and his wife had a Lexus that cost more than my first house. The payments on these two sweet rides totaled $1,800. His rent was $1,200. That's right: his car payments were more than his rent, and driving fancy cars was a bigger priority than being a homeowner.

He also had $30,000 in credit card debt and asked if the church wouldn't mind helping pay some of that off. Ha!

Since he wanted a quick, on-the-spot answer, I gladly gave him one, although not the answer he was expecting: "No," I said (and tempting as it was, I decided it would be un-pastorlike to lecture him that our faithful church members don't give their tithes and offerings to fund indulgent lifestyles).

"What do you mean, 'No'? You *have* to help me," he said. "If you don't make these car payments, my cars will be repossessed. I'm already two months behind!"

"Maybe they should be repossessed. You obviously cannot afford them," I said. I might as well have declared war and made fun of his hairline and his favorite NFL team in the same sentence.

"You don't get it!" he yelled. "I *can* afford these cars; I just don't have the money right now!" I seriously thought I was going to get punched in the face.

"Where do you work?" I asked.

"I'm an investor," he said.

"But *where* do you *work*?" I repeated.

"I work for myself," he said.

I was starting to feel like I was in a tennis match.

"And *where* do you work for yourself? Where do you go every day to do your investing?" I pressed.

"I work from home," was his answer. *Ding, ding, ding!* Houston, we have a problem.

"I would recommend you start looking for a job outside your home. You need to get a job with a paycheck that will pay your bills. And you need to sell those cars." I said.

Later that day, Andrew's wife called me to let me have it for refusing to help them. She was upset but at least rational, and I was able to get out of her some of the details of what led to the family's current financial state.

Two years prior, Andrew was working as a successful analyst for a military contractor. He made a good salary, just over $100,000 a year, and his wife stayed home. They didn't have any kids. A friend of Andrew's talked him into taking their savings and investing it in some invention a friend of the friend's just knew was going to go through the roof.

The gamble paid off. In two months' time, Andrew's $30,000 investment resulted in a $300,000 payoff. Andrew was hooked. He quit his job and upgraded their lifestyle with the cars, new clothes, and a few nice trips. Then he began devoting his time to finding the next big thing. Problem was, the next big thing never emerged.

Andrew was so sure he had "the magic touch" that he burned through the $300,000 in a matter of months and started borrowing on credit cards to fund new investments. Two years later, he was so desperate he was yelling at pastors for money.

A mature and emotionally healthy person would have taken the $300,000 windfall for what it was: a stroke of luck or a rare blessing. He would have likely paid cash for a modest home, bought a decent car or two, and enjoyed the spoils of a debt-free life. Just by investing his salary wisely and over time, Andrew could have—with relative ease—accumulated the millions he so obviously desired. But instead, he decided that he was some investment guru and developed an insidious counterfeit conviction that sullying his hands with actual work was beneath him. He fell into the seductive lure of quick money, and he went broke pursuing it.

But Proverbs 21:5 clearly states a timeless truth that could have helped Andrew immensely: "The plans of the diligent lead surely to plenty, but those of everyone who is hasty, surely to poverty." In other words, get-rich-quick schemes don't work.

You may be thinking, *Hey, but that guy* did *get rich quickly!* Yes, but was it ever *really* his, or was this just an opportunity for God to get his attention, an opportunity he failed to take advantage of?

Proverbs 20:21 says, "An inheritance gained hastily at the beginning will not be blessed in the end." And Andrew certainly didn't help matters by blowing through that money so quickly rather than setting up his family for success.

Where Is the Voice from Heaven?

While laziness, arrogance, and addictions keep a lot of people out of the workplace, for others, it's fear that has them sidelined.

Newly divorced Sophia Browning was definitely paralyzed by fear. Her father had made a killing decades earlier in timber, and her ex-husband was the wealthy owner of a car dealership. Still, while Sophia had never worked, she was intelligent, well-read, and well-educated.

She came to see me to get help improving her budget and reducing her spending. I had to hand it to her: for a woman who had come from wealth, she had done a bang-up job establishing a modest life for her new single self. She had a one-bedroom apartment and a used car, and she was using coupons to cut the cost of her groceries.

There wasn't much I could do to help her cut her expenses because they were bare bones already. And as modest as her expenses were, she was struggling for one significant reason: she had no income.

What she did have was determination to make it on her own. Her father had demanded she stay with her husband even though he was verbally and emotionally abusive. So when she left her husband, she cut all ties to her dad, and, therefore, his money. At thirty-eight, she was on her own for the first time, and she was ready for her independence. What she wasn't ready for, however, was a job.

"God hasn't told me to get a job," she explained.

"What? What do you mean He hasn't told you?" I read her the no-work-no-food passage out of Thessalonians, but she was undaunted.

"I didn't leave my husband until God told me to leave," she said. "I won't get a job until He tells me to."

"Did God tell you to brush your teeth this morning?" I asked. "Did He tell you to read your Bible? Did He tell you to put your car in drive in order to get here?"

"Of course not," she said. "I'm not some wacko; I just don't make major life decisions without hearing from God."

"That's commendable, but don't you think God communicates with us in many different ways?" I asked. "If you wanted to tell me right now that you had a headache, couldn't you communicate that in more than just words? You could put your hand on your forehead. You could pull some aspirin out of your purse. Is it possible that God is using your circumstances to direct you to the next place you are supposed to be?"

"I guess so," she said.

I shared with her one of my favorite passages, Proverbs 3:5–6, which reads, "Trust in the LORD with all your heart, and lean not on your own understanding; in all your ways acknowledge Him, and He shall direct your paths."

We talked about the different ways God directs us: through opportunities, encouragement from friends, dreams He puts in our hearts to go further and do more. Then we prayed together that God would give her courage and open doors for her in the job market. When we finished praying, she hugged me and said, "You know, I really am just afraid. I've never had a job before, and here I am, thirty-eight! What are they going to think of me? It's so humiliating."

And there it was—using "waiting on the voice of God" as a cloak for the fear she had in her heart. She had spent eighteen years married to a man who told her every day that she was useless and worth nothing, and listening to a father who told her that a good woman stays, no matter what.

"You've already done the hard part. You left. And you made it," I said.

"And God has been with me the whole time," she said.

"Look around you. Keep praying. Keep asking for opportunities, and see what God does," I said. "Keep me posted."

It wasn't long before I heard back from her. She had gotten a great job as a researcher at a local university. Her salary was more than enough to cover her expenses. She had hope and a brand-new future ahead of her.

> **Failing to work up to our full potential, is failing to live up to the person God created us to be.**

"God really does speak in all kinds of ways," she said. "I think I'll be a better listener now."

Refusing to work, or even failing to work up to our full potential, is failing to live up to the person God created us to be. Work is a gift from God. It gives us an outlet for our talents and creative energies, a place to connect with people of similar interests, and a chance to serve others by doing what God equipped us to do.

We simply cannot allow fear to get in the way of that.

I Really Hate What I Do

Quentin Sommers wanted advice on reducing his $80,000 in student loan debt. When we sat down together and evaluated his income, I was shocked to learn that this intelligent, educated, and attractive young man was only pulling down $16,000 a year. When I asked about his job, Quentin explained that he was working as a rock-climbing instructor and guide.

Quentin had a top-notch education from a good university and a degree in aerospace engineering. After some discussion, however, it became clear that while Quentin liked engineering, his real passions were rock climbing, sleeping late, and hanging out with his buddies.

Quentin and I had a long discussion about the goals he had for his life and what kind of income and lifestyle he wanted. (Far be it from me to discourage someone from living on beans and rice if rock climbing is what floats his boat.) Quentin did not want to remain a $16,000-a-year-guy. He wanted the rock-climber lifestyle on a rocket scientist's salary. That was not realistic. But it was clear from Quentin's choices that the lifestyle was winning out over the salary.

I outlined what Quentin would face if he went into default on his student loans. It wasn't pretty. Student loan companies can garnish a borrower's wages without even taking him to court. If Quentin's meager wages were garnished, even beans and rice would be out of his reach.

We reviewed Quentin's qualifications as an engineer. Turns out, he wasn't just your run-of-the-mill rocket scientist (if there even is such a thing). Quentin had a very unique specialization that was in high demand, and he sheepishly admitted that he could probably land a $300,000 job tomorrow. The problem was, the job would be at a certain company he didn't really want to work for, in Houston, where he had no desire to live. Quentin was only twenty-five. I asked him if he would be willing to put the mountain man lifestyle on hold for four years if it meant he could resume that life as a millionaire at twenty-nine. He said he could. I didn't even need a calculator to show him that in four years, he would earn $1.2 million before taxes. If he lived affordably and invested wisely while working as an aerospace engineer, he could pay off his student loan debt in a matter of months and amass a large cash cushion in a short amount of time.

Unfortunately, Quentin is taking his time putting his rock climbing shoes away. He is still teaching climbing lessons and leading tours and trying (halfheartedly, I suspect) to find a job as an aerospace engineer in a city that doesn't make him gag. Personally, I think I could sacrifice four years in Houston if it would make me a millionaire, but that's just me. You can lead a horse to water. . . .

But I Am Tweezers!

Another common hindrance to finding new employment is what I call the "one-trick-pony" mentality.

I have a friend who was laid off from her job as a newspaper reporter. She has lots of talents—graphic design, editing, photography, and she's a whiz with computers, just to name a few—but she cannot get her head out of the "I am a newspaper reporter" box.

As someone who has been in that same box, I can attest that it has very high and thick walls. People who have worked as journalists, especially if they were good at their jobs and genuinely cared about their work product, have a hard time ever seeing themselves as anything but a newspaper reporter. It's the same thing with police officers, artists, attorneys, educators, and other professionals with a strong sense of identity tied to their jobs.

The problem for my friend is that right now, there really aren't many job openings for newspaper reporters. And as talented as she is, when she finds an opening, she's competing with hundreds of other journalists for one slot, and it may not even be a reporting job that she would want to have.

Still, to look for a job as a photographer, graphic designer, or Web developer would be, in her mind, admitting defeat. And she's not ready for that yet.

When I have one-trick ponies in my office, I explain it like this: We're like Swiss Army knives. A Swiss Army knife is indeed a knife, but it is so much more. There are tweezers, a nail file, a bottle opener, a pick, an awl, pliers, and many other things, depending on which type of knife you have. You may have been tweezers your whole life, but if the job market is saturated with tweezers, you might find you need to try honing your pliers skills, at least for a while. And you never know; you may find that you enjoy being pliers even more than being tweezers.

The book of Exodus describes in great detail the building of the tabernacle and how different people played a part in putting the final product together. Some were called to work with wood, others with gold or jewels or tapestries. Some brought gifts to supply the materials for the tabernacle, and others supplied the labor to put it all together. But everyone had a part.

While none of us today may be inspired to "spin yarn of goat hair" (see Exodus 35:26), thank goodness, we all still have a job to do to build the kingdom of God. Exodus 35:31 says the workers were filled "with the Spirit of God, in wisdom and understanding, in knowledge and all manner of workmanship." God made us multitalented. Nowhere does it say that God ordained that Bill Smith will make ten shekels a day as a goat-hair weaver, and nothing else. It said that God gifted the workers "in all manner of workmanship." What they earned and when and how they used their gifts of workmanship were all in flux.

These people worked together to build one of the greatest houses of worship in history, and they didn't even have power tools. Surely Christians today can call on the talents God has blessed them with and be a little more open-minded in their job search.

It's hard for Christians to understand the ebbs and flows of life sometimes. When high-income jobs go away or other difficult financial seasons come, many believers automatically wonder if God is withholding blessings. But Ecclesiastes 3 makes it clear that there are seasons of ups and downs. Prospering in difficult times requires being flexible enough to adapt to change, and faithful enough to jump on new opportunities.

> **Prospering in difficult times requires being flexible enough to adapt to change, and faithful enough to jump on new opportunities.**

God has given us all special gifts and talents, things each of us is uniquely wired to do so we can provide for our families, enrich our lives, and bring glory to the One who created us. Why not get in the game?

Failing to engage to our fullest in the job market is inevitably symptomatic of something unhealthy going on in the heart. Are you afraid of failure? Are you struggling with addiction? Is a lack of humility keeping you from being a good employee and a helpful servant to your boss? Do you think you're too good to work, or just too good for a nine-to-five job?

Let your circumstances speak to you.

It's tough out there. I certainly don't fault people who really are doing all they can do to find work and still aren't getting the offer they're praying for. But if you've been laid off from your last five jobs, the only common denominator in each of those companies was you. So you have to be a grown-up and ask yourself what's going on with you that's causing the problem.

Are you unteachable? Uncooperative? Ungrateful? Unpleasant? Unkind? Uninspired? Unmotivated? Any combination of these will add up to unemployment.

Be strong, be brave, and get some help if you need it, but get out there. God designed you to do something fantastic and to be truly unique and amazing.

A prayer for your work life:

> Father God, I thank You for the gifts and talents with which You have blessed me. Please help me use these gifts to make a living for myself and for my family, to bless others, and to honor and glorify You. Break off any barriers in my heart that keep me from working up to my fullest potential. Give me a strong work ethic, energy for the day, patience for the tasks before me, and grace to handle my job with a smile. Bless the work of my hands, Lord, and please bless the job searches of everyone who is out of work right now.
>
> In Jesus' name I pray, amen.

God's Way

Here are the most important points to take away from chapter 4.

- When we have values for our lives that are important for us to uphold, our actions must support those values. We can't spend beyond our dreams.

- Laziness does not honor God; neither is it His plan for your life. However, God always blesses hard work and dedication.
- If it is important in your family that one parent stay home full-time with the children, it is imperative that you manage your money in a way that allows that to happen.
- God has promised that He will "never leave us or forsake us."
- Get-rich-quick schemes never lead to lasting wealth. And chasing the "next big thing" is not a valid excuse not to work.
- The Bible says that if you don't work, you don't eat. If you're physically capable of work, you should be working.
- Failing to work up to our full potential is failing to live up to the person God created us to be.
- Prospering in difficult times requires being flexible enough to adapt to change and faithful enough to jump on new opportunities.

Solution Steps

Here are simple steps you can take today to help you work—and earn—up to your full God-given potential.

1. List any values-based financial goals that you have for yourself and your family. For example, is it important for you that one parent stay home with the children? Do you want to send your kids to private Christian schools and colleges? Do you want to spend summers doing missions work overseas? Now take a few moments and pray about whether your current savings and spending patterns are supporting those dreams. What changes can you make today to ensure those goals become a reality?

2. Add up the cost of your goals and dreams. If mom staying home with the kids means $3,000 a month less in income, where will you make budget cuts to compensate? If you wish to retire at fifty to work with inner-city kids, how much will

you need at retirement, and how much more do you need to be socking away to make that dream come true?

3. Ask yourself if there are areas of your professional life where you are doing less than your best. If you are dissatisfied with your job, is it time to begin a job search? Are you not pursuing an area of talent because you're afraid of failure?

4. Take a few moments and reread Proverbs 21:5 and Proverbs 20:21. In the past, what have your attitudes been regarding get-rich-quick "opportunities"? How do you feel about them now? Highlight these verses in your Bible for easy reference when someone asks for your participation in a "sure thing."

5. Colossians 3:23 reminds us that ultimately, it is God that we work for. Print out this Scripture and put it over your desk at work to remind you that diligence and enthusiasm at work will be blessed.

6. If you just hate your job or the career path you have chosen, seek career counseling as soon as possible. Life is too short to toil away at a job you hate or pursue a path that doesn't feed your soul.

7. List the unique gifts and talents God has given you. Do you use those in your work? If not, are there ways to incorporate your gifts into your workplace?

8. How flexible are you when things change? When faced with a difficult new direction, list at least four possible ways you could respond and the anticipated outcome for each response.

FIVE

YOU MUST BE HERE TO HELP ME!

I don't know when and I don't know where it happened, but at some point in human history, there was a large convention of fine, upstanding Christian people. At this convention (I imagine it was at a large chain hotel, where everyone wandered around like dazed cattle with lanyards around their necks) the fine, upstanding people were gathered into a large ballroom with floral-printed carpeting and told the following: "Everyone in the whole wide world is here to help you! Everyone is good. Everything is safe. Skip through the daisies, and enjoy life, passing out dollar bills as you go." Those fine, upstanding Christians did go forth skipping through the daisies, flinging dollar bills in the air.

The world has been a breeding ground for criminals ever since.

Nowhere else on the planet does there exist a collective group of people as devoid of healthy skepticism as American Christians. As a whole, most of us think that anyone who walks up to us in church and shakes our hand is immediately to be trusted with our life savings, our children, and our fluffy little puppy dogs. There is no other explanation for why get-rich-quick schemes, multilevel marketing scams, insurance and real estate frauds, and various other sores on the financial world seem to not only persist but thrive behind stained-glass windows. I personally believe there is a very hot corner of hell (with

> Nowhere else on the planet does there exist a collective group of people as devoid of healthy skepticism as American Christians.

an endless loop of used car commercials playing at full volume) reserved for people who use the church to perpetuate their little financial schemes. But a lot of blame lies with the Christians who fuel their scams in the first place.

Frank and Melanie Connor came to me for help because they were facing foreclosure on their home. An investment property had already been foreclosed on, and they were falling behind on a $50,000 debt from a personal loan.

The real estate deals and the personal loan came courtesy of a pastor at their church. Pastor Shill, we will call him, convinced the Connors that he had a lock on a surefire deal that would help the young couple make a lot of money quick. They trusted Pastor Shill, so they bought the first property from a friend of—you guessed it—Pastor Shill's.

The second house was a dream home, for sure, but it was valued at more than double what they could actually afford for their home. But Pastor Shill assured them he could make the deal work. And work it he did. He had the Connors sign blank mortgage applications and promised to handle the rest. All they had to do was start packing!

While they were waiting for the closing on their dream home, Pastor Shill asked for a favor: he was trying to make another deal come together for another family, but he was short on the cash he needed to finalize the transaction. Would they mind taking out a $50,000 loan and giving him the money? He signed a promissory note agreeing to pay back the money, plus interest, in ninety days. It sounded like a sure thing, so the Connors signed.

After they closed on their dream home, the bank mailed them copies of all the closing documents, and the Connors discovered that everything Pastor Shill had put on the mortgage application was a lie. And the mortgage was an interest-only loan that in effect meant they owed more and more on the home every single month.

And it got worse. Pastor Shill stopped returning their phone calls and never paid back a dime of the $50,000 personal loan.

It was a mess of biblical proportions.

The Connors were worse than broke: they now had a foreclosure on their credit report and were quite certain they would be sued by the bank to pay the difference between what they owed and what the home sold for at auction. They faced another foreclosure on their primary residence, and they were saddled with $50,000 for a debt they took on for someone else, someone they trusted, who had no intention of paying back a dime.

Frank and Melanie had one of the most prevalent counterfeit convictions in the church today, and because of it, they checked their judgment at the church door.

Counterfeit Conviction: Because my intentions are good, everyone else's must be too. People who believe this assume that business opportunities presented by fellow church members, pastors, and other Christians don't need to be scrutinized.

Timeless Truth: God gave you a brain for a reason. If it sounds too good to be true, run! It doesn't matter who is making the pitch.

Jeremiah 17:5 says, "Cursed is the man who trusts in man and makes flesh his strength." And verse 7 says, "Blessed is the man who trusts in the LORD and whose hope is the LORD."

Trust No One?

This verse does not mean that we have to be like Mulder and Scully in *The X Files* and "Trust No One." Trust is so important that the Bible talks about it almost two hundred times. But most of those references are about trusting in God, with a few scattered warnings about trusting in man. What topic does the Bible cover twice as much as trust? Wisdom.

> **Trust is so important that the Bible talks about it almost two hundred times.**

Where trust and wisdom meet, good decisions are made.

Proverbs 4:7 says, "Wisdom is the principal thing." In other words, it is of primary importance to engage your brain.

We have to think about what someone is telling us and what someone is selling us before we whip out our checkbooks. It's common sense. And I wish I could say that there are no thieves in the temple, but there are. There always have been. And if you read Matthew 21:12–13, you'll see that Jesus didn't have much patience for them: "Then Jesus went into the temple of God and drove out all those who bought and sold in the temple, and overturned the tables of the money changers and the seats of those who sold doves. And He said to them, 'It is written, "My house shall be called a house of prayer," but you have made it a "den of thieves."'"

The people who came to church to do business—Jesus called them *thieves*.

So what does that say about a Bible study group leader who tries to talk you into joining his "network marketing" company? Or the Sunday school teacher who wants to sell you insurance? Or the pastor who tells you that the answer to your financial problems is a two-thousand-dollar software package, which—how convenient!—you can purchase from him?

Thousands upon thousands of Christians every year buy into this garbage, and it's wrong. There is one large church I know of where the entire congregation is fragmented into camps separated by which multilevel marketing company the members had joined. One group would not mingle with the other, and the biggest two groups certainly would not condescend to fellowship with the third, and Lord help anyone who went to a Bible study group connected with a different MLM company than their own.

What do you think Jesus thinks about all of this?

Now, let me be clear: I think there is nothing wrong with doing business with people you happen to go to church with. I do it all the time. In fact, I prefer to do business with fellow Christians because *most* Christians do things differently, with integrity, honesty, and a commitment to keeping promises. Notice I said *most*. This may shock you if you have a weak constitution, so get ready: there are crooked Christians out there!

Does this mean they're not really Christians? Well, no, because you may have noticed that there is no such thing as a perfect Christian. We are all at different levels of sanctification, that lifelong process of becoming more and more like God. Some of us are closer than others. Some of us are closer at different times of the day!

There are "Christians" who go to church every Sunday, read the same Bible, and sing the same songs you do, yet behave no better than a common swindler. It's not for us to judge their salvation, but it *is* for us to guard our wallets.

> There are "Christians" who . . . behave no better than a common swindler.

Here's another shocker. You may want to sit down for this one. There are people out there who will put the *ichthys* (the Christian symbol shaped like a fish) on their business cards, *who are not actually Christians!* The horror!

So how do you know whether you are dealing with a Christian businessperson or a wolf in sheep's clothing?

The people with honest hearts and the right attitude attend church to worship God and to serve and connect with others. They give; they lead; they volunteer. People who have the right intentions will only talk about what they do for a living as you get to know them personally. They separate their work life from their worship life and see church as a place to worship, not as a gold mine for potential clients.

Wolves walk through church with a stack of business cards in their pockets. Their eyes dart around looking for opportunities to network and cull potential clients. Their introductory handshakes are a little too firm. They don't give to the church, and they never volunteer unless it is to lead a Bible study group or teach a class. They will jump at a chance for those jobs because they see them as opportunities to have a room full of captives to hear product pitches. They're friendly for sure, but it is insincere. And they get to church real early: they want that primo parking spot in the front row so everyone sees the car magnets advertising their business.

A few years ago, a group of network marketers came to my church, wearing matching white T-shirts with "ASK ME HOW YOU CAN MAKE $20,000 NEXT MONTH!" in large, red letters. They sat in the center part of the auditorium and started handing out business cards.

Security escorted them out.

More recently, a guy came to church wearing a large electronic name tag that had scrolling and blinking letters advertising his business. He looked so ridiculous that I left him alone. I figured anyone who did business with a man wearing a blinking name tag deserved what they got.

So really, folks, if you engage your brain, it is *usually* not at all hard to determine which camp someone is in.

Some people at church want to tell you about their family and their relationship with God, and they want to hear about yours. Others hand you a business card within ninety seconds of the introduction. I call those "flaming business cards" because they're whipped out so fast, they get hot on their way to your hand, like a space shuttle reentering Earth's atmosphere. I get tons of flaming business cards. And you know what I do with them? I put them where they belong: in the trash.

Fleecing the Sheep

My primary job responsibilities are to teach financial classes, coach people with financial problems, and help them understand what the Bible says about money. Because I have access to people likely to purchase a financial product, I'm very popular with certain investment advisors, insurance salesman, mortgage brokers, and multilevel-marketing pitchmen. They make quite a show of sending me e-mails and promotional materials, or clogging up my Sunday morning with tales of how they can "help" our congregation or "take some of the burden" of my ministry off of me. Thanks, but no thanks.

I make a few wolves angry, but I protect my section of the flock like a shepherdess with a machine gun.

Understand, however, that church members cannot always count on their senior pastor, associate pastors, or anyone on staff to know every little thing that's going on. All church leaders—including Bible study group leaders, volunteers, Sunday school teachers, and more—have a responsibility to protect the integrity of the church. If you notice someone trying to take advantage of your fellow church members or using God's house for selfish gain, step up to the plate and call him out on it. Tell him to stop. Don't think for a second that you are stepping beyond your boundaries, because our churches belong first to God and second to all of us. Kick the wolves in the teeth. I promise, your pastors and fellow church members will be glad you did.

I do enlist the help of professionals from time to time. There is a wonderful woman who volunteers in my area of ministry who teaches portions of my classes that have to do with mortgages. She is a mighty servant of God, a faithful church member, and, yes, a mortgage lender. Why does she get that access? Because she's in the industry, and she knows way more about the changing mortgage market than I ever will. She's an expert. But she's a servant first. She has demonstrated over years of service that she will never create a conflict of interest by using her position in ministry as a way to get mortgage clients.

I met this woman when she took some of my classes and plugged in with my ministry by first asking how she could *serve*. And she meant it. What a concept. As I got to know her, not only did I notice how well she knew the Bible, how much she loved Jesus, and how deeply she cared about people but also she demonstrated a passion for helping people get the right mortgage and buy the right home. That's an important service to people, and that's the kind of person I want to partner with in my ministry. So, yes, she occasionally gets clients from me, but partly because she's never *asked* for them. I can trust her. I gleefully send homebuyers to her because I know her financial philosophy is biblically based. I also know that a few years ago, when interest-only, adjustable-rate mortgages were all the rage, she would have sooner eaten the mortgage papers than peddle such a financially devastating product. And I know she has integrity.

Same thing with the investment professionals that I bring in to teach our members about stocks, bonds, mutual funds, and the like. The people I pick for this role have integrity, and their primary focus is on *serving others*, not selling stuff.

And every one of them waited until they were *asked*. That's a big deal to me, and it should be a big deal to you.

Pastor Robert Morris of Gateway Church in Southlake, Texas, has a great line about the kinds of guest speakers he allows to preach at his church. He doesn't want anyone to come in and browbeat the congregation. "I want to bring in people who will feed the sheep, not beat the sheep," he says.

I agree. I also don't want anyone who's going to fleece the sheep.

Turning over the Tables

In my opinion, the two most egregious types of temple thieves are church members who invite others to a "Bible study" under the guise of trying to sell them something (that's just trickery) and pastors who use their position as a way to make a little hay on the side.

It's a conflict of interest, and it's wrong.

And here I am, selling a book, right? Well, far better pastors than me have written and sold books, tapes, CDs and DVDs, television shows, and more. But the godly ones pastor people first and use media as a way of spreading their message and helping others. It's not wrong for pastors to make money. We have to eat just like everyone else. It's not wrong for *anyone* to make money. But to take advantage of someone for a buck *is* wrong, and if you do so in a position of spiritual authority, God help you.

First Timothy 6:5 warns us to watch out for the "useless wranglings of men of corrupt minds and destitute of the truth, who suppose that godliness is a means of gain. From such withdraw yourself." In

> **To take advantage of someone for a buck *is* wrong.**

other words, run! Unfortunately, the world is filled with people who "suppose that godliness is a means of gain." And unfortunately, you have to watch out for them.

How can you tell? Matthew 7:15–16 says, "Beware of false prophets, who come to you in sheep's clothing, but inwardly they are ravenous wolves. You will know them by their fruits."

When ravenous wolves are nearby, there's usually some blood on the ground, so take a look around. If you suspect you're being approached by a wolf, talk to others who have done business with him or her. If the person is an employee of your church, talk to the senior pastor about what you've been asked to sign up for. If the peddler *is* the senior pastor, talk to a pastor at another church, preferably a church that is well known for its spiritual health. But most important, trust your gut and pray about it. Ask the Holy Spirit for wisdom and discernment. And if you're uneasy, don't jump just because the salesperson is a fellow Christian, a Bible study leader, or your pastor.

Think. And remember, if it's not okay to ask questions, there is a problem.

When I talked with Frank and Melanie later, they were quick to remember all the concerns they had in their dealings with Pastor Shill. "There were red flags all over the place. We would stay up late at night talking about it," Frank recalled. But, he said, Pastor Shill "really seemed to care about us. He even came to the hospital after Melanie had the baby. And we could tell he was making a lot of money outside of his job at the church, and he said he wanted us to have some of that 'blessing' too. We really thought he was the real deal. We thought he had some answers we were looking for."

"But it wasn't a blessing at all," Melanie said. "This whole thing has been a nightmare. And now, he won't even return our phone calls."

There wasn't much Frank and Melanie could do. They took my advice and went to the police, but ultimately decided not to file fraud charges against their former pastor, who had left the church soon after the Connors and several other church families lost hundreds of thousands of dollars.

None of those Christian victims of Pastor Shill's financial fraud pressed charges, therefore he has no criminal record of which I am aware. He's probably at another church by now, cooking up some new "business opportunities" and leaving more victims in his wake.

As for Frank and Melanie, after much prayer and consideration and after consulting with an attorney, they decided to ask their mortgage company for permission to do a short sale on the house. Fortunately, the bank agreed to accept whatever the house sold for as payment in full. The lien holder on the investment property decided not to sue, so Frank and Melanie ended up only being out $50,000, but they got a heartbreaking education in the process.

But Wait—There's More!

Christians seem more vulnerable than nonbelievers to liars and frauds outside the church walls as well.

I still shudder in horror when I remember the time I called my grandmother to check on her and she said she would have to call me back after "the nice man came down from the attic." She lived alone at the time, so I asked her who she had called and for what purpose. "Oh, I didn't call him; he just showed up at the door and asked if I would like him to check the attic seals," she said. "It's okay; he has a Christian fish on his business card."

Well, thankfully that business card didn't end up being a clue for the police to use to catch her killer. The guy tried to sell her new attic seals (whatever those are), and she said she would think about it. End of story, crime scene averted.

Maribelle Green's problem, however, was a little more complicated.

Maribelle was eighty-three and living off her Social Security checks, which didn't cover even her basic necessities. She was a very talented artist and was selling paintings on the side to try to earn extra money, she explained, because some months, she couldn't afford all of her medication. Late one night, while painting a landscape, she saw an infomercial about making money in real estate that sounded like a sure thing. She called the 800 number and—wouldn't you know?—the operator on the line was a Christian, too, and understood how hard it is to live on a fixed income. That was all Maribelle needed to hear.

Maribelle had a credit card that she saved only for "emergencies," but the nice and helpful lady on the phone convinced her to use that credit card to purchase a real estate seminar for $8,000. Now, in all of her eighty-three years, Maribelle had never left the state of Texas. And at that point, she needed help just to get to the grocery store. Yet somehow that lady managed to sell Maribelle a seminar in *Orlando*.

A few days later, Maribelle came to her senses and remembered that she could not travel and knew nothing about real estate. But when she called the company from which she had purchased the seminar to ask for a refund, they told her no.

Maribelle tried again and again for weeks to get her money refunded, to no avail. The credit card company was no help either since Maribelle was a competent adult who willingly made the purchase, and the seminar sales company had Maribelle on tape, acknowledging that she understood her purchase was nonrefundable.

By the time she asked for my help, she had all but given up hope. But I pulled out the greatest weapon I could think of: the threat of public humiliation. I called the PR firm that represented the company and laid out Maribelle's case. Was this something the PR company wanted to read about in the newspaper? The response was classic: "Sounds like we need to give her a refund." Bingo.

Three days later, the charge was removed from Maribelle's credit card, which she promised she would cut up into tiny, little pieces once she closed the account. As a thank-you, Maribelle sent me a lovely painting of hers that I now display with pride.

But what a shame she had to go through all of that. Maribelle was smart. She was tough. And she certainly wasn't greedy; she had legitimate needs. But somehow the promise of easy money and problems solved clouded her judgment and kept her from asking questions such as, "What do I know about real estate?" and "How am I going to get to Orlando?"

God Wants Me to Get Rich!

Many folks think there is a shortcut to quick riches. There isn't. That's why they call them "get-rich-quick *schemes*."

"The plans of the diligent lead surely to plenty, but those of everyone who is hasty, surely to poverty," is the admonishment of Proverbs 21:5.

> We all have seasons when we have plenty and seasons when we have less.

I believe Christians are particularly vulnerable to get-rich-quick schemes because of really harmful teaching that's commonly known as "prosperity gospel." Prosperity gospel teaches that God wants all of us to be rich, all the time, and that if you're poor, it means you don't have God's blessings on your life. That's baloney. We all have seasons when we have plenty and seasons when we have less, sometimes much less.

I've seen amazingly faithful Christians, people who love and serve

God with all their hearts, go through a season of one financial crisis after another, none of which were their fault. During those times they could always look back and see how God was with them and how He delivered them. And they came out of those hardships stronger than they ever had been before. Were they not blessed because they had difficulty? Of course not. It's just that difficulty is part of life. The wealth we build is a measure of our personal disciplines, our acumen with investing and money management, our ability to spend significantly less than we make, and our ability to earn.

Does a family of three, where mom is a hairstylist and dad an electrician, have much hope of becoming quick millionaires off their earnings? No, but if they save, invest wisely, and spend frugally, they can become millionaires over time. I know this family, and they are indeed millionaires. Happy ones. And you'd never, ever know that they have millions in the bank.

But what if they didn't save and didn't invest so well? Are they any less loved by God? Are they any less blessed? Of course not. People who don't do as well with their money are just as loved by God; they just miss out on the joy of being able to bless others and the peace and comfort that come with financial stability.

Prosperity gospel is a bad teaching. It twists the words of the Bible for selfish gain. Why selfish? Because a critical component of prosperity gospel teachers is that if you give to *their* ministries, God will bless you.

> I think God may well consider money the least of the many ways He can bless us.

There are many excellent ministries out there, and the good ones need your financial support. But honest ministers will teach you that the Bible says your first gifts, your 10 percent tithe, go to the local church. Tithing and caring for the poor, widows, and orphans are the only financial actions the Bible says are guaranteed to get God's attention and, in return, His blessings. But the Bible doesn't say in what form those blessings will occur. Personally, I think God may well consider money the least of the many ways He can bless us.

We live in a fallen world, and bad things can happen. Sometimes we do it to ourselves. That's what I did. Could God have intervened and stopped me from running up my credit cards? Yep. But He didn't. He let me dig myself into a pretty deep hole. But if I hadn't made that mistake, owned up to it, and turned it over to God, He wouldn't have used my mess and made it my message. I would not have had the opportunity to meet the thousands of people I have gotten to meet, teach, help, and pray with on the subject of finances.

That's the beauty of serving God. He can find your biggest glory in what you may think is your biggest downfall. He can take your ugliness and make it beautiful. The key is being willing to turn every aspect of your life over to Him. To trust only Him. To lean only on Him. When our faith is in God and not in man, or a plan, or a scheme, or a software package, wonderful things can happen in the face of great adversity.

One of the most amazing people I know is a man named Adam, a wealthy but humble designer of specialized computer systems. Not many people know what he does, or even who he is. He volunteers for some of the most unassuming tasks at his church. I was talking to him one day, and he mentioned "the time the kids and I were living in the car."

I had to ask how that happened, and I heard a story that rocked my world. His wife had gotten cancer and died, leaving Adam with three little children and staggering medical bills. She had no life insurance.

He had a good-paying job as a pharmaceutical salesman but lost his job shortly after his wife died. Out of work, and with more than $100,000 in debt, he would clean storage rooms and bathrooms at restaurants if they would let his kids eat. He soon lost the house in foreclosure, and for about a month, he and the kids lived in their car.

But this amazing man taught his kids how to worship God as they never had before while they drove around town with all their possessions in that car. "I tried to make it an adventure for them," he said.

"I never, ever once used the word *homeless*. It was 'Let's see where God takes us today!' even on the night when it got unseasonably cold and we had to use newspapers for blankets."

One day while he was bussing tables to earn food for his children, a patron at a nearby table struck up a conversation and invited Adam to drop by his office the next day for a chat. The man was a programmer, and when Adam visited him the next morning, the programmer offered him a job. He received paid, on-the-job training designing computer systems. Today, companies fly him to their headquarters all over the world to take advantage of his expertise. I would not even venture to guess how much he earns now. His kids are grown and thriving, and he's married to a beautiful woman who is just as sweet and humble as he is.

Would he have gotten where he is today without spending a very hard and heartbreaking month in his car?

The next time you have a financial setback or even a devastating blow to your life as you know it, resist the urge to wonder if God has stopped loving you, or if He allowed this to happen. Bad things do happen to all of us: it's not an indictment on your Christianity when things go awry. But trust that God has something amazing for you at the end of your journey. He does. I can guarantee it.

A Checklist

Because healthy skepticism and critical thinking are not often taught in churches, I offer here a checklist of things you should watch out for and consider before you engage in business with anyone, Christian or not.

1. When someone approaches you with a deal, an offer, or a business proposition, ask for everything in writing.
2. If that person attends your church, ask your senior pastor if any complaints have been lodged against him or her or about the "opportunity." If that person is on staff at your church, report the solicitation immediately to your senior pastor and

your church's elder board. If the solicitor *is* your senior pastor, you might want to consider finding another church.

3. Ask for references.
4. If there is any promise of quick wealth, a sure thing, or any other type of promise that you might have heard in a gangster movie, run.
5. Check any business with local and state agencies, including the Better Business Bureau and the secretary of state, for complaints.
6. Ask people who don't know anything about the "deal" to evaluate it and share their thoughts.
7. Pray about it. If you don't have peace, don't sign.
8. Don't buy anything, invest in anything, or attend anything you wouldn't if the person were not a "brother" or "sister in Christ." Business is business. It's preferable to do business with other believers, but doing business with your brothers in Christ is like clipping coupons: you don't buy stuff you don't like just because you have a coupon for it.

A prayer for wisdom and discernment in business dealings:

> Father God, please help me to have an open heart toward my fellow brothers and sisters in Christ. I do not want to be hard-hearted or cynical, yet I need help knowing when I can trust someone and when I should walk away. Help me understand people's motives and protect the resources with which You have entrusted me. Protect me, Lord, from people who do not have my best interests at heart, and keep me from people who would take advantage of me.
>
> In Jesus' name I pray, amen.

God's Way

Here are the most important points to take away from chapter 5.

- American Christians lack healthy skepticism more than any other group on the planet.
- Just because we have good intentions doesn't mean everyone else does. Business opportunities presented by fellow church members, pastors, and other Christians need to be scrutinized.
- If it sounds too good to be true, run, no matter who is making the pitch.
- Trust is so important that the Bible talks about it almost two hundred times. But God wants us to trust in Him first, and then in others, *after* we have done our due diligence.
- It's wrong to use the church simply to build a business.
- Church leaders, including volunteers, Bible study group leaders, pastors, and anyone serving in a leadership capacity, should be on the lookout for unscrupulous individuals out to fleece church members.
- Prosperity gospel teaches that God wants all of us to be rich, all the time. That's baloney. We all have seasons of plenty and seasons when we have less.
- We have to have a healthy level of skepticism when it comes to sales pitches and people who want our business. Be cautious with everyone, including your Christian brothers and sisters.

Solution Steps

Here are simple steps you can take today to help you be more discerning in your business dealings:

1. Play devil's advocate: list some reasons why someone might pursue Christians as potential customers. If you were not a believer, would you be inclined to think all Christians are gullible and trusting? Why is the church a magnet for scammers? What benefit would there be for an unscrupulous person to get his claws into a church body? When one side of your brain is thinking, *This doesn't feel quite right*, and the other side argues, *Don't be so cynical! He's a Christian! You can trust him*, use the list on pages 101–102 to help sharpen your discernment.

2. Does your church's culture encourage or discourage using the church as a marketplace? If you're uncomfortable with the culture, set up a time to talk to your pastor about it. Come to the meeting offering specific things you see and suggestions for how to change things for the better.

   Are you strongest in the area of trust or wisdom? Ask your spouse for his or her input before you decide. How does your strength in one affect your ability to use the other?

3. If you are a Christian businessperson who would like to do business with other Christians, consider the following suggestions for making professional contacts without crossing boundaries:

   • Offer information on your business only after a relationship has been developed and someone has asked you for information about your work.

   • Ask your pastor for suggestions on letting others know about your work in a way that's not pushy. How have others succeeded in this area? Under what circumstances does your pastor think networking at church is appropriate?

   • Post a business card or flyer on the church bulletin board. That's one way to get your message out without handing out "flaming" business cards.

- Serve first. If you're a faithful church member who serves others and builds authentic relationships, chances are you'll never have to speak a word about what you do. Let your service, your spirit, and your integrity do the talking for you. Do that and the business will come in a way that honors you *and* your church.

SIX

GOD IS AN ATM

I think giving can trip up Christians more than any other financial principle. On the surface, that seems silly. After all, what could be more simple than giving?

But we Christians have an uncanny ability to take the simple and make it complicated. To twist God's Word to suit our current purposes. To think maybe we've found a principle that applies to everyone else but us.

I'm going to make a bold statement here: you cannot be financially healthy without giving. Why? Because God created us in His image, and God is the ultimate Giver. The very idea of hoarding all we can for ourselves seems to fly right in the face of the nature of God, whose greatest gift was His only Son, who died on the cross so that we might receive eternal life rather than the judgment we deserve.

> You cannot be financially healthy without giving.

What if God had been selfish? Sobering thought, isn't it?

If the goal of Christians is to be Christlike, then why in the world would we ever be selfish? And why would God bless us if we were? Can Christians be financially healthy without giving? I don't think so.

But many Christians do try to follow Jesus without ever making the effort to bless others, and others give but do so for selfish reasons. Selfish giving? Isn't that a contradiction in terms? Not if you're giving only to get something in return.

The Bible tells us that giving falls into two categories: tithes and offerings. They are not the same thing. Tithing is the biblical principle of giving the first 10 percent of our income back to God through the local church. Offerings are gifts made over and above the tithe. There are many excellent books out there about tithing and giving, so I won't make all the theological arguments here for why we should. You're reading a Christian book about biblical financial values, so I will make an assumption that even if you're not doing these things already, you've at least bought into the concept that you *should* be doing them.

But if you're like many Christians, you could be thinking, *I can't pay all my bills, so how am I supposed to tithe? How can I possibly afford to give?* Those are good questions, so let's explore some answers.

First of all, understand that you're not going to hell if you don't tithe. Jesus' death on the cross was your ticket into heaven. If you've received Christ as your savior, your salvation is not the issue.

However, your heart *is* the issue.

Jesus Tax?

The first step toward being an effective giver is having the right heart toward giving, the right attitude. I've met with a lot of Christians who practically view tithing as some sort of "Jesus tax." Nothing could be farther from the truth.

> **A lot of Christians ... practically view tithing as some sort of "Jesus tax."**

What happens when we give is we are acting out an expression of faith that God has provided for all of our needs, just as He has promised. Now, if you have failed to effectively steward those resources, that's another matter, and we will address that later in this chapter. But just by stepping out in faith and giving, we're saying, "God, I trust You that what You've given me is enough." It's also an act of obedience. Proverbs 3:9–10 says, "Honor the LORD with your possessions, and with the firstfruits of all your increase; so your barns will be filled with plenty, and your vats will overflow with new wine." Everything in the earth belongs to God (Ps. 50:12). He entrusts us with a tiny portion of all that is His so that we may increase and multiply it (Matt. 25:15), care for our families (1 Tim. 5:8), and bless others (Matt. 25:40; Deut. 15:7–8).

So if you decide to give as an act of faith and obedience, you're halfway there. But you're still missing the most important component of a healthy giving attitude: cheerfulness. In 2 Corinthians 9:6–7, Paul wrote, "He who sows sparingly will also reap sparingly, and he who sows bountifully will also reap bountifully. So let each one give as he purposes in his heart, not grudgingly or of necessity; for God loves a cheerful giver."

Are you a cheerful giver? I have to admit, this is one area where I personally struggle. I have to pray and ask God to help me have a generous heart. Generosity comes naturally to some people. It's a beautiful gift, like having a magnificent singing voice or being able to paint, because when your joy comes from blessing others, you have the capacity to create something more beautiful than anything that exists on canvas.

But just as one person may be gifted with an exquisite singing voice while another person is not, the person without the gift of singing can usually at least be taught to carry a tune. You can develop a gift for giving the same way: step out in faith and give; then step back and see how it looks, how it feels. Over time, you can begin to create something truly beautiful.

In 2005, Scott and I started using the cash envelope method of budgeting, using envelopes containing the exact amount of money we planned to spend on regular expenses like groceries, gasoline, clothing, and incidentals.

In late August of that year, Hurricane Katrina hit New Orleans, and many residents were bussed to other cities for safety, including Fort Worth, where I was working as a newspaper reporter.

One day, at the beginning of September, I went to a local hotel where FEMA had rented rooms to house some of the displaced families that had been relocated to Fort Worth. I was walking down a dimly lit hallway, searching for families that might be willing to talk to me, when I heard an incredible sound. It was a woman's voice, and she was singing.

"What a friend we have in Jesus, all our sins and griefs to bear. What a privilege to carry everything to God in prayer."

I followed the sound of her voice until I came to the open door of one of the hotel rooms. There, amid clothing donated by strangers; food from local churches; and bland, chain-hotel furnishings, was the source of the song: a woman folding clothes, surrounded by nine children, ranging in age from about five to seventeen.

She welcomed me in and introduced her grandchildren, all of whom had been separated from their parents but somehow managed to find their grandmother and end up in her care. The children were silently sorting through the donated clothes, setting aside what they could use and carefully folding other items to share with other families in the hotel. Most of the donated food was prepackaged, microwavable meals, but the family had no access to a microwave. Their homes and all their worldly possessions were gone, and yet, they were smiling and singing, gracious and grateful.

The spirit of the woman and her grandchildren was impressive. There was no complaining, just gratitude that they were safe and together. She smiled the entire time we spoke. I was so moved by her faith and so very aware of her needs that when I finished my interview with her, I reached into my purse and pulled out all of the cash from my budgeting envelopes. She tried not to take it but relented when I said, "It's God's anyway, and He wants you to have it."

I knew everything was God's, and I was just a steward of a small portion, but in that moment, I really felt in my heart the full truth of what that means. It was the first time I had full knowledge that God had entrusted me with something—that cash in my wallet—that was *actually meant for someone else.* I was just the courier.

That was a pivotal experience for me. Before 2005, I only paid with plastic. Even after we stopped the credit card cycle, I still preferred my debit card to cash. But if I had not had those cash envelopes that day, how could I have helped that woman?

I have no idea how much I gave her—certainly not much, maybe a couple hundred dollars at most—but frankly, it doesn't matter. The blessing I received from that moment was worth ten times more than what I gave away, because in that moment, God showed me the power and the joy of spontaneous giving.

The other significant way this experience changed me was that it was God's way of showing me how joyful it can be to give. I had been praying about giving and asking God to help me in that area. Like the father of the afflicted child in Mark 9:24, who cried out to Jesus, "Lord, I believe; help my unbelief!" I was trying to have faith. And I was giving—but not really enjoying it. I had asked God to give me a heart to enjoy the process. Writing checks to your local church and institutions you believe in is important, for sure, but if you do nothing but write checks, you're distancing yourself from the emotional benefits of giving. Want to give with joy and passion? Get involved. Nothing ignites the flame of giving in your heart like directly meeting the need of a total stranger. Nothing will give you more joy when you give to your local church than if you are also actively involved as a volunteer.

Make a donation to the local food pantry. But instead of dropping the check in the mail, hand-deliver it; then spend an hour or two stocking the shelves or sweeping the floor. Watch as families in need come to pick up their food baskets. That will certainly get you excited about helping others.

At our church we have a special class for people who are in the direst financial circumstances. The students in this class are people who lack resources to even pay rent or buy food for their families. They are desperate and hurting.

During one class, a single mom shared how she had received an unexpected fifty-dollar tip from a customer at the restaurant where she worked as a waitress, and she told the group how excited she was that God would bless her in such an unexpected way. As she was sharing her story, her eyes fell on another woman in the class. While the waitress didn't know it, this other woman was facing even tougher circumstances. The waitress said that she felt the Holy Spirit tell her that the fifty dollars was actually for the other woman. So after class, she pulled her aside in the hallway, and handed her classmate the cash.

"I had been asking the Lord to give me some money that I could give away and help others, and He did!" the waitress said later.

In my own encounter with the woman from New Orleans, I realized that while I had written a lot of checks, I had never considered the importance of physically connecting myself to the act of giving. But after praying about it, God gave me the connection my heart had been craving.

There are three ways we can give: our time, our treasure, and our talents. I think it's a pretty wimpy worldview to give with your time and your talents, but not your treasure. Your local church cannot pay the light bill with your talents, glorious as they may be. I've encountered more wimpy Christians than I care to number who say, "I don't tithe, but I give my time to the church, which is even more valuable!" Oh, please. Even if they did give a tenth of their time every week to their church (which would be, by the way, 16.8 hours), if everyone had the same idea, the church would have to shut its doors. How can churches give to the poor, pay for educational programs, and keep the water on to flush the toilets if no one gives?

> I think it's a pretty wimpy worldview to give with your time and your talents, but not your treasure.

Volunteering is important, but so are monetary contributions. Luke 12:34 says, "For where your treasure is, there your heart will be also." If your treasure is not in God's house, your heart's not there either.

God Is My ATM

At the other end of the giving spectrum are the give-to-get folks. These people give, all right, but they do so with the misguided assumption that they can manipulate God into blessing them because they gave. They twist the words of Luke 6:38: "Give, and it will be given to you: good measure, pressed down, shaken together, and running over will be put into your bosom. For with the same measure that you use, it will be measured back to you." They put money into the offering plate, fully expecting to retrieve from God more than they gave, like some sort of heavenly slot machine. It doesn't work that way.

> Giving with the right attitude and a generous heart *will* be blessed.

God will bless a cheerful giver, one who gives generously with the right spirit, expecting nothing in return except the joy that comes from blessing others. That's a biblical promise. Giving with the right attitude and a generous heart *will* be blessed. But God doesn't promise exactly *how* those blessings will come.

I've heard stories of people making sacrificial gifts and then getting a check in the mail days later for the exact amount they gave. I'm sure it's happened, but that's the exception and not the rule. And it's certainly not a reason to give one penny to any church, person, or cause. You give because you want to give, because you're grateful for all God has done for you, because it's the right thing to do. Regardless of your circumstances, there is always someone who has it worse than you do, and blessing him or her even in the midst of your own need is a powerful thing.

I've never received a magic check from giving, and I would venture to guess that you haven't either. Am I blessed? Absolutely. But not in a way that any late-night televangelist would flip his toupee over.

Here are the blessings I know I can count on when I give:

- My money goes farther. When I carefully plan out a monthly budget, giving my tithe off the top of my income, the other 90 percent goes farther than if I had never given at all. Happens every single time.

- Things seem to last longer. Stuff doesn't break as much. Purchases go the distance. I don't know if I could scientifically prove it, but I'm convinced my car gets better gas mileage and a bottle of Tide lasts twice as long.

- I have divine favor. People are constantly amazed at the deals I get without even trying. If I've been saving up for a beautiful metal wall planter for my front porch—BAM!—the thing will be half price once I save up the money and go online to order it. Or the very thing I need will pop up on Craigslist. Or a friend will casually mention that she is about to get rid of something that happens to be what I've been looking for.

- I have peace. I know I have God's blessings on my finances because I've been obedient and given with a cheerful heart. That eliminates a lot of worry. I know my budget is lined up with God's will because I've given first. Everything else is just details.

But giving to God, then immediately asking, "Okay, where's my blessing?" shows a greedy, irresponsible heart.

Another question I get a lot has to do with tithing on gross income versus net income. Again, this gets back to the fact that Jesus is after our hearts, not our wallets. It's a heart issue. If you're giving 10 percent of your net income with a grateful and cheerful heart, I believe that's a better reflection of God's desire for us than if you're reluctantly giving 10 percent of your gross. It goes back to 2 Corinthians 9:7, which we first read in chapter 1: "Let each one give as he purposes in his heart, not grudgingly or of necessity; for God loves a cheerful giver."

I once had a couple break into a loud argument in my office because she was angry that they weren't tithing on their gross income. That's not the spirit of giving, my friends.

Personally, I think it's good to err on the side of generosity. When we get to heaven, I don't think Jesus is going to slap anyone on the back and say, "Good to see you! But why were you giving 3.2 percent more than you had to?" So if it's a choice between gross or net, go for gross if that's how you feel "purposed in your heart." The important thing, though, is just to give.

One Blessing, Please, and Charge It!

Betsy Morgan was giving to get, not because she was greedy, irresponsible, or evil, but because she had bought into a version of giving that sells God as that supernatural ATM.

She came to see me about her $7,500 credit card debt. That's not a lot by today's standards, but Betsy's only income was Social Security, so her debt was a huge problem. She attended a very small church, but someone had told her about my financial ministry at the "big church" nearby, so she asked if I would help her.

When the seventy-two-year-old widow came to see me, I had her bring in her credit card statement. The problem was immediately apparent. She had charge after charge listed to a television-based ministry. Betsy was ready for me though: she brought with her a copy of a magazine article called "The Big Blessing Revolution!" written by the head of the ministry to which she had been giving. He was one of those give-to-get televangelists—you know, the ones who jump up and down, screaming and yelling promises that Jesus Himself will knock on your door with one of those Publisher's Clearing House–sized checks if only you'll give to this TV ministry. Gag.

She had written proof (or so she thought) that her credit card gifts were her ticket to unlimited blessings. I sat there and read the article until my stomach turned.

It went something like this: "God wants to bless you in a mighty way! God has millions! Billions! Don't you want what's yours? You can have it if you get on board with what God is doing! Are you on board with what God is doing? Are you funding the work of His ministry? Don't lose your blessing! Give today!"

I would be surprised if the exclamation point on the guy's computer keyboard hadn't fallen off from overuse. The article was a disgusting piece of garbage, much like this guy's TV "ministry," but Betsy bought it hook, line, and sinker.

I set aside my anger at the televangelist and asked Betsy about her giving. She truly did want to be a blessing to others, but she could not tell me one thing this guy's particular ministry was doing other than entertaining her on TV. But she had connected with the televangelist and was fully confident that God would bless her if she blessed his TV show. Make a little deposit in the First National Bank of God and have unlimited access to the ATM at the back of the building.

I beg to differ.

I think that in any circumstance, we can look at the product of our actions to determine if God's blessing is on them. All Betsy had was a pile of debt, sleepless nights, and frustration.

"Betsy," I asked, "From where are you getting the money to give to this ministry?"

"My Visa card," she said. "You can see it right there."

> We can look at the product of our actions to determine if God's blessing is on them.

"And do you have the money to pay off this bill?" I asked.

"No," she said. "That's why I'm here."

"So you're using Visa's money to fund this ministry?" I said.

She wiggled in her chair a bit before answering, "I guess so."

"So would you reason that if this televangelist is right, and there's a blessing coming from giving money to him, Visa is going to be the one to get that blessing?"

"I hope not!" she said.

"But you're giving money you don't have, money that's not yours. And you expect to be blessed from that?" I said.

"Well, that's what the preacher said," she explained. "God is my only hope. How am I ever going to get out of this debt if God doesn't bless me?"

I explained to her that going into debt to chase a "blessing" wasn't biblical and wouldn't work. You can't trick God into blessing you, and you don't need to. God wants to bless us, and He wanted to bless Betsy; she just had it all wrong.

Her spiritual catch-22 was confounding, and she didn't even see it. She was going into debt to give to a ministry and by doing so she thought God would bless her with the resources to get out of the debt she was incurring to give to the ministry. (Say that fast a few times and see how long it takes to get a headache.)

Counterfeit Conviction: Giving is like a magic wand. I can spend recklessly and neglect to save because giving will prompt a blessing from God that will make all my past stupidity disappear.

Timeless Truth: Giving is a critical component of any healthy Christian's finances. However, in order for giving to be effective, it must be done with the right attitude, the right spirit, and in conjunction with saving, hard work, and smart money management.

"Giving is a wonderful thing, but not if you are going into debt to do so," I said. "It is going to take hard work, sacrifice, and a lot of prayer to pay off this debt. I want you to give, but I want you to give money that's yours, and I want you to start by giving to your local church first. Then, once you are out of debt and you have more money to give, you can start looking at giving beyond your local church to other ministries. But I want you to find ministries that do work you are passionate about."

Betsy loved children, so we did a little research and came up with three ministries that helped orphans and underprivileged children in the United States and abroad. That got her excited to have a plan: with a little hard work and some right thinking, she could soon truly be a blessing to others.

She was already watching her grandchildren for two hours a day after school until her son and daughter-in-law came home from work, so I told Betsy to tell them about her debt and ask for payment for her services. She resisted at first, but she called me later to say that her son was more than happy to pay her ten dollars an hour for babysitting. That generated four hundred dollars a month to put toward her debt. She started tithing to her local church out of gratitude and obedience, not expectation, and the stress of the past few months began to melt away. She also began volunteering in the children's ministry of her church and doing volunteer work in the office, helping the pastor maintain his files and return phone calls.

Six months into her new financial journey, Betsy got her blessing in the most unexpected way. Her pastor preached a message on tithing and asked her to share her story with the congregation.

It was painful to admit to the 150 people in the church that she had been giving to get, but she shared her story and received a standing ovation when she held up her wish list of ministries she planned to support once her debt was paid. A few days later, there was an envelope bearing only her name on the desk she used outside the pastor's office. Inside was a check for five thousand dollars and a letter from a church member thanking her for her service to the church and instructing her to use the money to pay off the last of her debt.

I continued to meet with Betsy for a while when she was still paying down the debt, and in the course of our conversations, she admitted she was lonely before her grandkids came over, so she watched televangelists to pass the time. We worked on her budget and reduced some of her expenses so she could tithe to her local church. Then we devised a volunteer schedule that she was comfortable with, that kept her working in her church and blessing others, eliminating any chance of becoming bored or lonely. Not only did Betsy no longer have time to watch the dollar-a-holler guys on TV, she lost all desire to tune in to them because through tithing and volunteering, her heart and her passion were back where they belonged, in her local church.

I Can't Afford to Give

A lot of Christians say they would like to tithe, but they think giving is for the rich. "I'll tithe when God gets me out of debt," they might say. Or, "I would be such a great giver if I had a million dollars!"

> A lot of Christians say they would like to tithe, but they think giving is for the rich.

It's like a version of spiritual algebra: If God does X, then I will do Y.

No, you won't.

God has already blessed you. If you can't give out of your current resources, don't fool yourself into thinking you would give if you had more, because you wouldn't, and you can't fool God into thinking that you would.

Mark 12:41–44 describes Jesus' reaction to the widow who gave two small coins, "her whole livelihood." Jesus was so impressed by her gift that He called the disciples over to take note of it.

In Luke 16:10, Jesus said, "He who is faithful in what is least is faithful also in much; and he who is unjust in what is least is unjust also in much." In other words, if you can't budget, plan, save, and give on $35,000 a year, you won't be able to do it on $350,000 a year either. Think I'm wrong? Elton John, MC Hammer, Donald Trump, Nicolas Cage, Cyndi Lauper, Marvin Gaye, Kim Basinger, Toni Braxton, Zsa Zsa Gabor, and Burt Reynolds are just a few celebrities who went broke or even filed bankruptcy even though they made far, far more than that. *Sports Illustrated* found that 78 percent of NFL players are bankrupt or close to it within two years of retirement. And 60 percent of NBA players are broke within five years of retirement. Money

management skills do not rise propor-
tionally to increases in income.

If you want to give, you *can* give.
Starting today. You may have to make
some changes, and you may have to
make some sacrifices, but you *can* give,
regardless of your current circumstances.

An ideal spending formula is 10-10-80.
Give the first 10 percent, save the second
10 percent, and live below your means on
the rest. Easy as pie, huh?

> **Money management skills do not rise proportionally to increases in income.**

Now, if you are currently spending 20 percent more each month
than you bring home, you have a problem. You'll have to make some
radical changes to your spending habits in order to bring things into
balance. Can you start with 10 percent? Maybe, but probably not, at
least not right away. When I'm coaching people in this situation, I go
through their budgets with them and make cuts until spending is less
than income.

The first month or two that a chronic overspender is on a budget,
a good ratio to shoot for is 1-1-98. You have to start somewhere, and
giving 1 percent, saving 1 percent, and living on the rest is certainly
better than living beyond your means.

If you make goals to keep looking for cuts and reducing your
spending each month, you could realistically shoot to improve your
ratios by 1 percent a month. So the next month would be 2-2-96, and
so on. Allowing for a hiccup here and there, a reformed overspender
could be giving 10 percent, saving 10 percent, and living well on the
rest within a year.

Is that a difficult process? Absolutely, but it is worth every ounce of
effort it takes. Going from worrying about bills to blessing others, saving for the future, and having wiggle room in your budget is a feeling
like no other. And anyone can do it, regardless of his or her circumstances. *Anyone.*

By outlining a plan to start at 1 percent, I am not at all saying I think giving 1 percent is the biblical ideal. I'm saying that I personally believe God gives us grace and time to get from where we are to where we need to be. Is 1 percent ideal? No, but it is better than nothing, and if giving 1 percent is part of a financial recovery plan that gets you to the ideal of 10 percent in about a year, I believe it's a great first step that will help you spiritually, emotionally, and financially while honoring God at the same time.

> Most people who say they can't afford to give are hiding behind their overspending as an excuse to be selfish.

I think most people who say they can't afford to give are hiding behind their overspending as an excuse to be selfish.

Occasionally, however, I will counsel someone who has a real gift for giving and finds his greatest joy in blessing others, yet he doesn't have the money to give as he would like to.

These folks usually fall into two camps: The first group simply doesn't manage their money. They give and give but have no budgets and no financial plan, so they don't have enough money for their own needs. This group often has some serious faith issues because they walk around wondering why God is not meeting their needs, when in fact, He has met their needs; they just didn't plan an effective use of their resources.

The second group consists of the rare few who budget and plan their giving in accordance with their budgets, but they truly just want to give more. They are genuinely grieved that they cannot buy a van for a missionary who needs one or cannot pay off the mortgage for a struggling single mom.

To these folks I have two suggestions. First, take heart: God doesn't expect us to give beyond our means. When the disciples became aware that a famine would strike Judea, Acts 11:29 says that each gave "according to his ability," to aid the people there. Even the disciples were of varying financial means, and they gave different amounts.

Second, if you're really passionate about meeting a need or aiding a cause in greater measure than what you can do on your own, martial other resources. Get friends to pitch in and match your gift. Have a fund-raiser. There are other ways to generate support for an important cause than simply opening your own wallet. Give according to your ability, then trust God to do the rest.

God is the ultimate Giver. He sets the standard for demonstrating generosity toward others because He gave the greatest gift, His Son. If giving doesn't come naturally to you, ask God to create generosity in your heart and to give you opportunities to share your blessings with others in a way that will make giving more joyful. If you love to give but find you don't have the resources to give as you would like, ask Him to help you steward and plan better, so you will have the resources available to bless others when the opportunity arises.

A prayer for giving:

Father God, I understand that You want us to be generous givers, and I wish to give in a way that honors and glorifies You. God, show me the people You would like me to bless. Let me see clearly the needs of those who are less fortunate than I am and give me compassion for them. Help me to manage my money effectively so that I may share the resources You have given me with others, so they may know the goodness that comes from loving and serving You. God, thank You for the spirit of generosity. Unlock generosity in my heart in fresh and new ways, and let me love others the way You love me.

In Jesus' name I pray, amen.

God's Way

Here are the most important points to take away from chapter 6.

- You cannot be financially healthy without giving.
- Tithes and offerings are not the same thing. Tithing is the biblical principle of giving the first 10 percent of our income back to God through the local church. Offerings are gifts made over and above the tithe.
- When we give, we are expressing faith that God has provided for all of our needs.
- God wants us to give cheerfully, with grateful hearts.
- When you get personally involved with the people you're blessing, giving becomes more personal and joyful.
- It's a pretty wimpy worldview to give with your time and your talents, but not your treasure.
- God will bless us for giving with the right attitude and a generous heart, but He doesn't promise exactly how those blessings will come.
- Giving to God, then immediately asking, "Okay, where's my blessing?" shows a greedy, irresponsible heart.
- In any circumstance, we can look at the product of our actions to determine if God's blessing is on them.
- God has already blessed us. If we can't give out of our current resources, we need not think that we would give more if we had more.
- Money management skills do not rise in proportion to increases in income.
- An ideal spending formula is 10-10-80. Give the first 10 percent, save the second 10 percent, and live below your means on the rest.
- If you've been living beyond your means and you can't immediately give and save 10 percent, start somewhere, even if it's only 1 percent. Don't overspend as an excuse not to give or save for your future.

Solution Steps

Here are simple steps you can take today to help you and your family have a healthier attitude about giving:

1. Pull out last year's tax return and examine your charitable giving. How do you feel about the amount you gave? More important, what do you think God would say about your giving? Were you generous and cheerful in your gifts? Were you stingy and begrudging? Or did you not give at all?

2. Examine your budget and determine what percentage of your income you are actually giving every year. Do you think you should reduce spending in other areas so you can give more?

3. Pray about your attitude toward tithing. Do you believe it is a biblical principle? Why do you think God wants us to tithe? Discuss this question with your family to determine if you're all on the same page regarding your giving.

4. If you don't naturally have a gift for giving, find a way to get personally involved in a cause you care deeply about. Personal connection is more meaningful than just mailing a check, and may help you understand the purpose in your giving.

5. Draw a pie chart of all of your giving: time, treasure, and talents. Are you satisfied with the percentages?

6. Have you ever wrestled with a give-to-get mentality? Pray about God's desire for your giving. Make a list of the ways God has blessed you for your generosity.

7. If you're not giving 10 percent of your income, or anything at all, try to begin adjusting your spending and expenses over a period of time to allow for giving and savings. Both are equally important for your financial future.

SEVEN

THE SCARLETT SYNDROME

Scarlett O'Hara from *Gone with the Wind* is one of my all-time favorite literary and movie heroines. The sheer ferocity and tenacity with which she devoured her life is one part inspiration and two parts cautionary tale, not unlike my own life, for sure. One of her best lines in the movie comes when Rhett Butler asks her a troubling question. Her classic response, "I'll think about that tomorrow," is ingrained in the psyche of many a broke individual. Many of us are all about having fun today, leaving the cares of life for "tomorrow." But tomorrow gets put off until the next day, or the next day, or until Miss Scarlett hits the wall. In the book and in the movie, this attitude is one of the characteristics that makes Scarlett so charming and such an engaging character. But in reality, it's no way to live. The modern-day Scarlett's life is a mess.

> **Many of us are all about having fun today, leaving the cares of life for "tomorrow."**

The thing about Scarlett is that she can be hard to spot. A Scarlett is just as easily male as female, and the one characteristic you can count on in the life of every modern Scarlett is that she (or he) looks really good on the outside.

Scarlett is a top earner in her field. She is well respected, and she works hard—she has to in order to support her lifestyle. She will have a nice house and dress well. And you can bet she drives the best car on the block. Vacations are nonnegotiable, and they're not the car-and-camping sort, either.

She also talks a good game. You will think that her 401(k) is maxed out and that she's on the fast track to pay off her mortgage. She reads financial books and magazines and doles out advice to which people pay close attention. When she gets an idea, it's generally a good one, and she goes after it with gusto. Then, in an instant, she has another idea, and she's off after something else.

Scarlett is one of the most creative people you know. She seems fearless and tough. She's usually in the middle of some sort of drama, but it's always of the entertaining variety that you tend to talk and laugh about over lattes, which she pays for. You notice that Scarlett uses plastic—a lot. But she's smart, and you just assume she knows what she's doing.

Everyone likes to be around Scarlett—most of the time. She's usually the life of the party. She knows the best restaurants and the best places to shop, yet she loves to quiz her friends in search of new places to go and see and things to do and buy.

But occasionally Scarlett gets moody. Without warning, storms brew over Scarlett's otherwise sunny horizon. She gets crabby and reclusive, and you may not hear from her for a while. Then, without warning, she's back, sunnier than ever.

Yes, Scarlett looks good on the outside. But here's what's brewing under the surface:

Her lovely home is mortgaged to the hilt. Her car is leased. She knows all about investing, retirement savings, and the best options offered by her company's 401(k) plan, but she doesn't participate because she needs every dollar to keep her lifestyle afloat. The clothes and vacations, lattes, and restaurant dinners were all charged to one of her many maxed-out credit cards.

Scarlett's sunny life is built on a house of cards that's always on the verge of collapse. What Scarlett's friends don't know is that her occasional moodiness is due to the house of cards falling down. She will disappear while she concocts a quick fix, usually by borrowing money from yet another source to placate one of her creditors; then everything's okay again. For a while, anyway.

Sunny-Side Up

Some of the characteristics that make Scarlett such a fascinating character also contribute to her struggles. At the top of that list: her optimism.

Scarlett's glass is always half-full. Things tend to work out well for her because she expects them to, which means she is always caught off guard when things don't go as planned. Not getting a counted-on raise or promotion can send Miss Scarlett into a tailspin, often because she had already spent the anticipated additional income. While enjoying her sunny day, she always counts on an even sunnier tomorrow, and she makes risky and expensive bets that her life is just going to keep getting better and better and her paychecks bigger and bigger. Such an outlook on life seems, to a casual observer, consistent with Christian principles of faith and positivity. After all, Philippians 4:8 reads, "Whatever things are true, whatever things are noble, whatever things are just, whatever things are pure, whatever things are lovely, whatever things are of good report, if there is any virtue and if there is anything praiseworthy—meditate on these things."

> **Hope for the best, but plan for the worst.**

Doesn't that seem like just the sort of scripture Scarlett would have on her fridge?

But we also have a warning in Matthew 5:45: "He makes His sun rise on the evil and on the good, and sends rain on the just and on the unjust." In other words, we have to hope for the best, but plan for the worst. Yet Scarlett would rather put her fingers in her ears until the bad stuff goes away. But life doesn't work like that.

Scarlett has to guard herself because her greatest assets, her drive and her positive outlook on life, also feed her counterfeit conviction and create a cycle of living on the edge of posh poverty.

Counterfeit Conviction: I can leverage tomorrow's blessings to make today even more fabulous, because my next windfall is just around the corner. Everything will be fine and if it's not, well, I will just worry about that tomorrow.

Timeless Truth: It rains on the just and the unjust. Need another example? How about Noah? Genesis 6:9 tells us that Noah was a "just" man who "walked with God." In fact, he was such a good guy that he stood out before God as the lone man worth saving in a fallen and corrupt world. Noah was *that* good. And yet, who got more rain than Noah?

Failing to account for things not going as planned is foolish and will have any would-be Scarlett forever playing catch-up in his or her own life.

I have counseled many, many people with this counterfeit conviction. And this is one of my favorite personality types to counsel because I know the way Scarlett thinks, I know how she acts, and I know how to help her. How do I know? Because I *am* her. I have a recurring theme in my life of always seeing only the up side of life and not looking for things failing to go as planned. Generally speaking, that's a pretty healthy outlook. It only becomes unhealthy when we allow ourselves to feel derailed when things don't go as planned. That's my weakness. I'm always shocked when things don't go well, and I handle upsets badly. Sometimes it's as if I'm thinking, *How dare life throw me a curve ball?* That's a very shortsighted and arrogant view of life. We have to expect difficulties.

One recent evening my husband and I were both lamenting an unusually stressful day, so we decided to pile our three boys in the car and go out for dinner. Scott and I were still so entrenched in the difficulty and setbacks of the day that we didn't talk much during dinner, which was Mexican food capped by chocolate sundaes for the kids. The kids were just picking up their spoons to dive in to the gooey goodness when Addison, five, demanded, "Hey, shouldn't this sundae have a cherry on top? Where is the cherry?"

I chided him for his lack of gratitude but chuckled under my breath that he inherited such a strong version of his mother's worldview.

"Ice cream, good! Hot fudge, good! But where's my stinking cherry?" I wonder how often God watches me and has the same reaction I had to Addison. I wonder if He ever thinks, *Hey, woman! Look around you. So, things aren't perfect. How about expressing a little gratitude for the sundae? Not everyone has a sundae, you know.*

I have believed in the power of gratitude since I was a child. Unfortunately, I also picked up a gift of pointing out what's missing. Not so good.

Scarlett always notices if the cherry is missing, and she allows the "loss" not only to tarnish her enjoyment of the sundae, but to cause her to make reckless decisions to compensate herself for what's missing. Here are some ways that plays out in life:

"I had a crummy day at work, my best friend is mad at me, and the house is a mess. I deserve something nice. I think I'll go buy a new outfit. I don't have the cash, but I'll just put it on my credit card. I deserve it, after all!"

"The light bill is due, but these cute shoes are on sale, so I really should buy them now. I'll worry about the light bill next week."

"That's it! I'm done putting up with this jerk of a boss. I'm quitting. So what if I don't have another job lined up—I'm so smart that employers will be lining up to hire me!"

"I need a vacation. I don't really have the cash for it right now, but that's what credit cards are for. My performance evaluation is due next month, so I'll just pay off the bill with the huge raise I am sure to get."

"Yikes—my credit cards are all maxed out. I'll just take out a loan from my 401(k). I'll figure out how to pay it back somehow."

"The payment for this new car is only $150 more a month than my current car payment. I can swing that. I've been spending too much on groceries, anyway."

See the pattern? Scarlett can always talk herself into spending more and more, forgiving herself for sabotaging her budget if she's compensating for some perceived slight or loss. It's a toxic habit. And while her optimism knows no bounds, her income certainly does. Sooner or later, her habits catch up to her, and the crash is painful.

In Denial

Some people with this counterfeit conviction aren't necessarily reckless or neglectful with their money; they just have a tendency to stick their heads in the sand when it appears things might be going south. They will ignore scary circumstances even when doing so is clearly to their detriment.

Harold Marshall had this problem.

This dear man came to me because he had a collection no one would covet: for months he had been stockpiling—but not opening—letters from the IRS.

He had been praying for weeks that God would resolve the matter without him having to do anything. But every day, there the letters remained, piling up on his desk. He came to see me for prayer on the matter, and I suggested we find out exactly what we were praying about. Harold protested for quite a while. He put up a really good fight. But I showed him Psalm 143:8, a prayer to God, saying, "Cause me to know the way in which I should walk." Then I told him, "Harold, this verse indicates that we need to know *exactly* what we are dealing with." He relented, and one by one, I opened the letters.

The news wasn't good: Uncle Sam wanted $45,000 in back taxes from three years prior. Harold lost it. I've never seen a grown man cry so hard.

But once the shock wore off, Harold admitted that he wasn't entirely surprised, and that opening mail wasn't the only thing he had delayed taking action on. He hadn't filed a federal tax return in many years.

It wasn't that Harold hated paying his taxes more than anyone else, and he certainly knew that in Matthew 22:15–21, Jesus outright tells us to pay our taxes. Harold, however, was somehow of the belief that if he ignored the problem long enough, it would either go away on its own or that he would get to it . . . eventually.

Obviously this was not a good game plan.

I recommended two first steps: First, some serious prayer time, and second, a phone call to the IRS. (I always recommend prayer, but it is particularly important when one is about to contact the IRS.) I unlocked an empty office so Harold could have some alone time with God. I suggested he repent for ignoring the problem and for failing to pay his taxes and ask for God's grace and mercy over the whole situation.

Harold had a lot to pray about. Delay in financial matters is seldom a good idea, but in Harold's case, it was particularly costly: the fine the IRS was seeking had increased significantly every month he delayed.

After an hour alone in prayer, Harold picked up the phone and called the IRS. God smiled on him that day, and the IRS employee who took his call was helpful and sympathetic. He helped Harold set up a schedule of affordable payments, and Harold gave a time frame for when he would file the other missing returns. I gave Harold the number of a good CPA so he could get caught up on his tax problem and help him make sure he never ignored his taxes again.

> **What we put off until tomorrow is generally much more costly than if we had addressed it today.**

Harold will spend much more time and significantly more money cleaning up his tax problem than he would have if he had just taken care of it to begin with. That's almost always the case with financial matters. What we put off until tomorrow is generally much more costly than if we had addressed it today.

Fortunately, Harold was able to get a good-paying second job. He committed all the income from that job toward his tax bills, and he resolved never to delay important financial matters again.

Helping Scarlett

One of the more interesting aspects of my job is that while all the people I coach have consistently similar financial problems, half come to the table overwhelmed by feelings of failure, lack, and loss, while the other half essentially ignore their spending issues until the credit dries up, creditors start calling, and life starts falling apart. So throughout any given day, I wrestle a poverty mentality out of some folks, and with the other hand, I fight a devil-may-care attitude with another group. The devil very much does care, and he probably dances with glee at the way some incredibly bright and talented people manage to mess up their money and their lives by refusing to maintain a realistic outlook.

The key word here is *realistic*. I'm not talking about being pessimistic, but neither am I talking about being overly optimistic. Somewhere between the two is a happy little place called *cautious optimism*.

One of the key ways I help Scarlett is to lead her to discover the freedom of cautious optimism, and the shortcut to that happy place is an understanding of the difference between optimism and denial. I start here because when I hit the wall in my own financial life, much soul-searching revealed that this was a key place that I veered off the road of financial health and into crazy debt.

If you are a Scarlett yourself, getting this difference down will be of paramount importance to your financial health. Let's explore.

Let's say Scarlett's boss tells her that the company has had a great year and that she will be getting a year-end bonus of $1,500. Woo hoo! Scarlett will have spent the money in her head before she leaves her boss's office. Not only has she made the decision on where the money is to go, but she's also likely to whip out the plastic and go ahead and buy the thing, expecting to pay the bill off when the bonus comes. Furthermore, she will treat herself, or her kids, hubby, or home, to a few other nice surprises, rationalizing that she can afford it since she's getting that bonus.

Before the bonus even hits her bank account, Scarlett has probably spent that $1,500 at least twice, if not three or four times, and likely gone into debt to do so.

Scarlett's in denial. She's denying the fact that $1,500 is just $1,500, no more, and doesn't enable her to spend $3,000 or $4,500. She's in denial that things can go wrong with an anticipated bonus. The accounting department may suddenly discover that the company is not doing so well after all and that they may even need to consider pay cuts. Or she may suddenly need some really expensive dental work. Or the transmission might be due to clunk out in her car right around the time the bonus would be kicking in. Any number of things could go wrong, but Scarlett's not considering any of that. In her mind everything's smooth sailing as far as the eye can see. In fact, this one little blessing is causing a chain reaction of happy thoughts prompting her to spend and spend and spend.

A cautiously optimistic approach would be to thank the good Lord for the expected bonus and then do nothing until the check actually lands in her manicured little hands. Nothing. No planning or scheming or plotting of any kind until the check actually arrives. Then and only then should she consider the best use of the money, based on her current circumstances and her long-term goals.

I will never coach someone on the best use of money that he or she does not currently have. It's one of my more irritating characteristics as a pastor, and I know I've annoyed more than one person who has called me about similar expected windfalls.

CALLER: Hey Pastor Amie—I'm getting a raise! What credit card should I pay off first?
ME: Wow! That's great! When are you getting it?
CALLER: Oh, in about six weeks, when my promotion kicks in.

ME: Awesome. Call me in six weeks.

CALLER: What? Why? Why can't I decide now?

ME: Because you're spending money you don't have yet. That's never a good idea. In fact, you're asking for trouble. Bye!

Proverbs 16:9 says, "A man's heart plans his way, but the LORD directs his steps." It's good to have a plan, but don't execute the plan until all the pieces are in place. You never know when God might have another plan for what's ahead.

> Spending a windfall you don't yet have . . . is like waving a red cape in front of a bull who's having a bad day.

There are three things you can do in life that will invite trouble every time: flirting when married; developing an affinity for any food that is fried, cheesy, or creamy; and spending money you don't have. Spending a windfall you don't yet have, even in your head, is like waving a red cape in front of a bull who's having a bad day. You may escape without being gored, but why bother? Just don't do it.

Twists and Turns

Another way I help Scarlett correct her behavior is to help her admit that she's an adept manipulator. Once she admits she's good at manipulation, I can help her recognize when she's doing it. But it's a tough sell.

No one wants to admit he or she is a manipulator, least of all a high-minded Scarlett. But think about it: Scarlett usually stumbles when she manages to talk herself into a purchase with skewed reasoning, when on a deeper level, she knows good and well that it's not okay. If you can lie to yourself, you can bamboozle just about anybody.

Manipulation is a form of deception, and just a hiccup or two away from out-and-out lying. The hard part for Scarlett is that she's been doing it so well for so long the behavior often creeps up unnoticed.

But creep up it does. Back to the bonus example, first Scarlett convinces herself that it's okay to go ahead and spend the money since the bonus is coming anyway. Next, if she's married, she has to convince her spouse (or rather, explain it, since most Scarletts I know, male or female, would have already made the purchase before they got home).

Let's say Scarlett bought a new laptop with the money. The laptop was $1,299 (she's a Mac girl). But the computer came with a "free" (after rebate) printer for $150, and she needed new software, which added another $300. Throw in a new computer bag and tax and she's actually spent about $2,000.

When she gets home to show her new laptop to her honey, you can bet that thing didn't cost a penny over $1,299. And the price may have even gotten magically downgraded (or rounded down, that is) to $1,200 in the retelling. She doesn't mention the software, the printer that was "free," and the bag that has somehow decided to spend the next couple of days in the trunk of her car until the heat dies down.

You can't tell me that's not manipulation. And it may seem "cute" or "funny," but a lie is a lie is a lie. And if Scarlett is carrying debt from month to month, it's a lie that's killing her family's finances (and most likely eroding the trust in her marriage). It's not worth it.

If a Scarlett is repeating this behavior over and over again, then someone close to her is allowing it. She's found herself an enabler. Mine was my wonderful, darling husband, Scott. Scott thinks I hung the moon. He thinks I am beautiful and funny and that everything I do is pretty cute. He still thinks this after fourteen years of marriage, God bless him.

But the truth is there is nothing cute about being childish and deceptive with money. While I can't recall ever doing this particular type of manipulation over a computer, I did it with lots of other things, and Scott let me get away with it. In fact, I was so good at "spinning" my purchases and weaving tales of miraculous sales that when I would come home from shopping, Scott would greet me with, "How much did you save?"

One of the most powerful things we did for our marriage was for me to call out my own behavior to my husband and then ask him to help me stop it. I not only gave him permission to ask me tough questions, I made sure he understood that he wasn't doing his part as my husband if he didn't. And I made a promise that I would stop twisting the numbers and manipulating the details to buy something I shouldn't have.

It took a lot of maturity on both our parts, and it took a few months to get the process down, but we did get it down.

Here are some of the steps we implemented to help us stick to our budget and slay the shopping spin doctor:

1. Before I went shopping, we discussed what I planned to buy and confirmed that the cash I would be spending was budgeted.
2. Any purchase over our set amount (back then our benchmark amount was twenty dollars) that had not been previously discussed warranted a phone call.
3. I never went shopping just because I was bored or I felt like shopping, and I didn't buy anything we hadn't previously agreed that we needed, even if it was on super mega once-a-year sale.
4. I shot straight about what I spent. No fudging the numbers.

Now, this may sound like the hammer came down, and suddenly I had to go asking permission to buy diapers and coffee filters. But it wasn't like that at all. For the first time, we simply started acting like grown-ups. We started communicating openly and honestly about money and needs and wants.

I personally believe that when we are blessed enough to marry the person God designed for us, when the pastor says, "I now pronounce you husband and wife," from that point forward, God sees us as one. Genesis 2:24 says, "Therefore a man shall leave his father and mother and be joined to his wife, and they shall become *one flesh*" (emphasis added). So I see Scott and me as two individual halves of one pretty amazing unit. When we work together, using the best that each of us has, there's little we can't do. When we go it alone, the results are usually pretty comical, and not in a good way.

Scott is, by nature, financially conservative. He's the saver. He's also not a detail guy. He wants the big picture only. You've probably surmised by now that I am a spender. Money used to burn holes in my pocket. I love the details, and I love to shop. I love to hunt for the best bargains and figure out how to make a deal work. But by not asking enough questions, because he doesn't care about the details, Scott was letting me shoot us in the financial foot every time I went into a store. He let me lie to myself and manipulate him.

Scott doesn't *want* to ask questions, but he does now because he knows we do better together when he is involved. I know he is looking out for what's best for our family when he does ask those questions, so I offer up all the details, ensuring we can make good decisions together.

Hair-Trigger

Another characteristic of Scarlett, and yours truly, is that she is impulsive. She will come home with something she doesn't know how she ever lived without, even if she hadn't heard of the thing before she walked into the store. She's a bulldog when she decides she wants or needs something, and she won't release her grip until she gets it. She will go from decorating the house to planning a European vacation for the entire family without stopping for coffee. She's hard to keep up with.

Male Scarletts are the kind of guys who go to the electronics store to get a DVD and come home with a new home theater system. Or they leave the house on Saturday morning in a minivan and come home that afternoon in a sports car. "Go big or go home!" is the rallying cry of the male form of this species.

Male or female, the impulsiveness of this particular personality type certainly contributes to the financial sabotage, but at the same time, it is their greatest asset when they finally do decide to ditch the debt.

That's right: impulsiveness is your friend when it comes to a financial turnaround.

Why? Simple. Impulsive people make decisions quickly and then tend to stick with them. Convince them that something is a good idea and they will take the idea and run with it and never look back. Other personality types put more thought into their decisions, and change is harder for them. That plays out for a lot of the broke people I counsel when they have difficulty changing their behavior, even once they are convicted that change is for the best. Many broke people waste years of hemming and hawing and coming up with a million silly reasons why now is really not the best time to grow up and stop leveraging their future. They cling to their counterfeit convictions like *Titanic* passengers to a lifeboat. They hang on to bad behaviors for years and have a really hard time making the hard decision to start being smart with their money.

> **Impulsiveness is your friend when it comes to a financial turnaround.**

But woe to anyone who stands in the way of an impulsive Scarlett who has made up her or his mind to change. Once the switch has flipped, it's a done deal. Scarletts are the first ones in line to shred their credit cards in my classes because they are the first to buy into a different way of handling their money. They attack their debt with a fervor most often associated with football fans. You better just get out of the way.

So take heart if you're learning that Scarlett is your middle name. You may have dug yourself into a deep, dark financial hole, but you also have the strength and tenacity to climb out.

And after all, tomorrow is another day.

A prayer for Scarlett:

God, I'm so sorry that I've been unrealistic about my finances, in denial about my choices, and manipulative in my spending. Help me see my finances clearly and make good choices. Lord, I am also sorry that I have been dishonest with myself, with You, and with others about my spending. Please help me stop this behavior today. Help me use the gifts You have given me to handle my money with maturity and wisdom in a way that will bless my family and honor You.

In Jesus' name I pray, amen.

God's Way

Here are the most important points to take away from chapter 7.

- It's not responsible to think only of having fun today and engage in reckless financial behavior, deciding that we can leave the cares of life and the consequences of overspending for tomorrow.
- People with the Scarlett Syndrome look great to the outside world, but in reality, their finances are a mess.
- We have to hope for the best but plan for the worst.
- We can't expect that the next windfall is just around the corner. Leveraging tomorrow's blessings for today's pleasure will only lead to financial failure.
- The Bible warns us that it rains on the just and the unjust. Just look at Noah.
- Don't use life's shortcomings and disappointments as an excuse to "reward" yourself by buying things you don't need and cannot afford.
- It's healthy to be optimistic, but nobody's life is perfect. We

have to expect that difficulties, trials, and tribulations will
come from time to time.

- We also have to be cautious about sticking our heads in
the sand when things get tough. We can't ignore scary
circumstances when failing to take action can harm our
finances.
- What we put off until tomorrow is generally much more
costly than if we had addressed it today.
- Cautious optimism strikes a healthy balance between optimism and pessimism.
- Don't spend money you don't yet have.
- Caution yourself against being manipulative when it comes
to spending money, talking about money, or making spending decisions. Be honest!
- If you have an impulsive nature, use it to your advantage!
Formulate a debt-elimination plan, and don't look back.

Solution Steps

Here are simple steps you can take today to help you and your family
balance the wants of today with the needs of tomorrow:

1. For every financial decision, list the best-case scenario, the
worst-case scenario, and a likely outcome in between. Before
you make up your mind, ask yourself if you can live with the
worst-case scenario. Don't just assume things will work out
the way you want them to.
2. In every situation, hope for the best, but plan for the worst.
3. If you're having a bad day, are feeling sorry for yourself, or just
have the blues, *do not go shopping*. People with the Scarlett
Syndrome have a tendency to rationalize reckless spending
as a way to make themselves feel better. It's a trap. Don't fall
into it.

4. Make a firm decision to never again put off until tomorrow that financial thing that you really need to do today. Every day you delay will only add to the cost and frustration of getting the matter resolved.
5. List ways you can begin practicing cautious optimism—then do it.
6. Decide today that you will never, ever spend money before you have it, even in your head.
7. If you have Scarlett tendencies, ask your spouse and closest friends to hold you accountable to not be manipulative in your decisions or your conversations about money. Make a promise to yourself to tell it like it is and not paint a rosier picture that will trick you and others into thinking you are spending less than you actually are.
8. Set a trigger amount that you and your spouse can agree on. If either of you wants to spend more than, say, fifty dollars for something that was not budgeted, it warrants a phone call from the store or a conversation at home before the purchase is made.
9. Use impulsiveness to your advantage. Make a decision *today* to do better with your money, and stick to it.

EIGHT

THE CLIFF JUMPERS

The sweet people in my office were clearly confused, as was I.

Derrick and Susan had been married for twenty-six years, and much of that time was spent laboring in ministry, serving others. They raised three great kids, worked hard, lived all over the country, and had absolutely nothing to show for it. In fact, they had crippling debt, the kind of staggering debt load that would torment the sleep of any rational person: more than $150,000. Their annual income was around $30,000. There were tears and many sleepless nights.

In talking through their life in ministry and the choices they had made, they were confused about why things had gotten so bad. They were intelligent and careful in so many areas of their lives. How did this happen?

Like most couples, Derrick and Susan didn't find themselves in a mess overnight. It was the slow accumulation of many, many bad choices, compounded over time, multiplied by inaction and denial.

Bankruptcy wasn't even an option, as most of the debt was to the IRS and student loan companies (loans obtained on behalf of one of their children) and personal loans that Derrick was determined to honor.

They came to me to formulate a plan, but I was stuck on the "how." How in the world did they get here? Derrick and Susan were not crippled by any of the usual counterfeit convictions. They had tithed their whole lives. They didn't fall prey to any tricks or schemes. They hadn't done any one outrageously stupid thing. They worked hard. But time after time, when decisions really mattered, they made the wrong choice, often a reckless one, even after prayer and thoughtful consideration. It was a life pattern, consistent for them, but inconsistent with every other area of their life.

For weeks, I was stumped.

I helped them devise a communication plan to their creditors and to start making token payments on what accounts they could, but I knew real breakthrough wasn't coming for them or for me until I could understand what happened in their lives to cause this kind of financial breakdown.

About three months later, I found myself in our church's café one Sunday morning, talking with Derrick and Susan, along with another couple that needed prayer and counseling for debt problems. I was sharing with the couple a rough outline of what the Bible says about being careful with your money. It was sort of a scriptural argument for being financially conservative, all the time.

And that's when Susan interrupted me. And the lightbulb went off for all of us.

"But, Amie! We weren't taught to think that way. I agree with you, *now*, but you have to understand," she said. "That's not what we've been taught."

Derrick and the other couple nodded in agreement.

"What do you mean?" I asked.

"We've been taught that if you don't go so far out on a limb that only Jesus can save you, you don't have any faith," she said.

And—ping! There went the lightbulb.

"But . . . but . . ." I stammered, stunned. "That's the stupidest thing I have ever heard! What if the limb you've climbed out on is not the limb God had for you? What if you're wrong? What if you do something stupid out of your own will and then just put God's name on it? (A common Christian practice.) Then what?"

"I guess that's why we're all in the boat we're in now, Amie," Susan answered. "Nobody ever asked those questions. We thought it was all about our faith."

She explained that they had been taught that great faith walked hand in hand with great risk, that if you weren't consistently making enormously risky leaps of "faith" with your life, you weren't really living life "more abundantly," which Jesus told us, in John 10:10, He came to earth to give us.

To me that seemed like such a skewed and dangerous teaching, one that could lead only to Christian families having their lives repeatedly falling into shambles. Kind of like the two families I was talking to in the café that day.

I was reeling. I was angry.

And I was kind of relieved.

Now it made sense. But I had tons of questions—was this a denominational difference? A common teaching? Or some freak coincidence that both couples had heard and practiced this fallacy most of their adult lives? And how could any pastor in good conscience teach people that reckless behavior is a sign of solid faith?

While I was raised in a denominational church, these other four folks all spent most of their church lives in a nondenominational setting. The difference? Christian denominations have standardized teachings—*doctrines*, in church lingo—that don't vary from church to church. When you sign up to be a pastor in a denominational church, you agree to teach according to the beliefs of the denomination.

Pastors in nondenominational churches have no such rules. There's freedom in that (No dancing? Why? It's in the Bible!) but also a bit of danger if the pastor sees the Bible more as a list of "suggestions" than something to model a life after.

Still, even nondenominational churches tend to fall into groups that have a lot of common teachings. And these two couples from different parts of the country attended churches that taught this same principle. They didn't question it. They lived it. And the result was devastating.

Understanding the Cliff Jumpers

I had to know more, so Susan and I started e-mailing back and forth about their counterfeit conviction. One e-mail summarized their experience like this: "One ministry we were associated with quite early on in our marriage held the belief that faith looked like getting out there so far that only God could get you where you were going or bring you back. Otherwise your faith was not as strong as it could be. The only option without a miracle was failure, and that was seen as strong faith and very spiritual."

Wow.

The practical equivalent of their behavior goes something like this: Imagine having an impulse to jump off a cliff. You pray about it, and with the absence of an audible voice from heaven saying, "Don't jump!" you decide God wants you to jump, never mind the people behind you yelling to back away from the edge.

Next imagine diving headfirst into the abyss, without getting a parachute, a helmet, or even a Band-Aid first, then asking God why He didn't catch you when you hit the ground.

Often we make reckless, life-altering decisions with the same amount of care and planning.

> Confirmation is the difference between following an impulse and answering a divine calling.

I believe that God sometimes asks us to make big changes. Sometimes part of His plan involves a career change, a cross-country move, a bone-rattling investment, or a sacrificial gift. But I also believe that God gives us confirmation along the way so that if we slow down long enough to look for it, we can find bits and pieces or sometimes glacier-sized hunks of evidence that we are on the right path. Confirmation is the difference between following an impulse and answering a divine calling.

The Bible tells us that there is wisdom in a multitude of counselors. In 2 Corinthians 13:1, Paul wrote, "By the mouth of two or three witnesses every word shall be established." Heeding the wisdom of the smart people around you (not the nut jobs who can't manage their own lives but somehow seem to know exactly what you need to do with yours) is like a safety net in case you get too close to the edge. Listen to wisdom and you will bounce right back.

So let's explore the counterfeit conviction at work here. While the elements of carelessness and recklessness are obvious, I think there's more to it than that.

For cliff jumpers, the counterfeit conviction is compounded by a tendency to attach God's nature to one's own impulses and whims.

Counterfeit Conviction: My every impulse to do something bold is a divine calling from God.

Timeless Truth: Sometimes God does call us to take bold leaps. But you have to have the maturity and discernment to know when something is God and when it's just your impulses flaring up.

> To ascribe God's name to the chaotic fallout of a personal choice goes against the very nature of who we know God to be.

The Bible shows us in great detail just how methodical and orderly God is. He is the author of math, the calendar, weather patterns, and the rotation of the planets and solar systems. He is not random, and He is so much bigger than any human experience. To ascribe God's name to the chaotic fallout of a personal choice goes against the very nature of who we know God to be.

Here's another way to look at it: Imagine I sat down and wrote this book in one sitting. I didn't, of course, but imagine me sitting down and typing constantly over hours and then days, writing and writing and never once hitting the Save button until I finished. Does that make any sense? What if while I was writing, I kept praying and having faith that nothing would go wrong? What if while I was typing, I looked up and told you, "I have faith that God is not going to let anything go wrong with my computer!"? Would that at all change the likelihood that the software program wouldn't lock up, that the computer wouldn't crash, that the cat wouldn't jump on the keyboard and accidentally step on the Delete key?

Would that be wise? Of course not. That's why we hit the Save button often and have backup hard drives and other methods to save our work. That's not lack of faith; it's common sense.

When God Says "Stop"

Years ago, right after my twins were born, I had a very strong desire to open a boutique in downtown Fort Worth. I love clothes and thought I could really make a go at a successful business. I found the perfect location, wrote a business plan, and presented it to a development company. I had even culled a top saleswoman from a high-end department store who had a Rolodex of every lunching lady in the Dallas–Fort Worth area, customers who could keep us prospering for decades. The development company loved my ideas and wanted to invest—heavily—with one catch: they wanted me to quit my reporting job and run the boutique myself full-time.

In my head, everything seems to say, *Do it! This is your chance! Chase the dream!* But my ears were filled with the cautionary screams of friends who thought I was headed for disaster.

"There are empty storefronts for a reason. Don't start a boutique in this economy!"

"You really want to give up journalism for retail?"

"Do you have any idea what kind of hours are involved in running a boutique? I know you don't want to make that kind of time commitment with a four-year-old and twin babies."

I listened. I paused. I prayed.

In the end, I used the very best decision-making gauge I believe God has given us: peace.

As in, I had none.

Even just thinking about quitting my reporting job would cause my stomach to start churning like a washing machine. My sleep became sporadic. I became irritable and fretful. But my head was still hung up on the possibility of the opportunity, so I kicked my research into the viability of emerging specialty retail into overdrive.

And then, I stopped. I decided to make a trial decision to pull the plug on that dream.

I slept like a baby that night. And the next day, I put the boutique plan to bed, once and for all.

Now, granted, we all have friends who think *everything* is a bad idea. They are full of tales of woe of all the bad things that can happen if you fly that airline or fail to buy this certain product for your home. God bless 'em.

But we all generally have at least two or three friends who unconditionally believe in us, encourage us, and pretty much think we can do anything we put our minds to. When those friends start waving red flags, you're an idiot if you don't listen.

When God Says, "Go"

Here's another example that went a different way.

When I was offered the position of financial stewardship pastor at New Life Church in Colorado Springs, I had never even been to Colorado before the job interview. I had a great job at my home church in Texas, a home I loved, in a neighborhood surrounded by friends, a pond, and a playground for my boys. All my family and most of my friends were a car ride away. My universe was secure.

Then the offer came.

My stomach did handsprings, but I slept.

My oldest, Cole, who was seven at the time, suddenly abandoned his protests and was on board with the idea. And while we were initially baffled as to what Scott would do for a job and his income if he left his newspaper reporting job, freelance writing opportunities started pouring in. I began seeing Colorado license plates all over the place—in Fort Worth. I would overhear strangers talking about ski trips, mountain hikes, and trout fishing.

My mind was clear. My prayers were deep. My sleep was peaceful. My heart was still.

Instead of accusing me of being a few bricks shy of a load, friends started asking, "Are you really going to go?"

Now, don't get me wrong: I was scared. I didn't really know anyone in Colorado, and the church had some major baggage that I was walking into as a total outsider. I was heading into a complete unknown. So again, after much discussion with Scott and many hours of prayer, we made another trial decision. We were going.

Peace washed over me like a tidal wave.

It was still scary, but good scary. Bumpy, for sure. Moving with three little kids, a dog, a cat, and your whole life in U-Haul trucks is not an experience I care to repeat anytime soon. Maybe ever.

But when I woke up that first morning and blinked toward the uncovered window of our new home and saw the mountains, I thought, *We made it. This is right.*

We knew.

We stepped out in faith, but we received layer upon layer of confirmation that our steps were in the right direction. Our income was secure. We found the right place to live. Friends encouraged us. People in our church felt strongly that we were making the right decision.

And we have been blessed here ever since.

Was it perfect? No, because we're not perfect. But when I counsel people who've moved here impulsively and without jobs, I'm tempted to make a list of all the warning signs they failed to heed. No job, no place to live, no prospects, no support from friends or family, just a desire and a strong inkling that "God told me to move to Colorado." None of that was the case for my family.

The God Stick

I'm always wary of the "God told me to" declaration. At my church, we call that the "God stick" because people usually like to use those words to bully someone else into submission, usually to support their bad decision. Like the woman who showed up at our church, demanded to see a pastor, and then insisted I hand her at least six hundred dollars in cash, on the spot.

When I started asking questions, I found out that she had purchased a new refrigerator for that very amount the month prior, and the expense had put her in a financial bind. She didn't attend our church, but I suggested, hypothetically, that if she had called me and asked me if she should buy the new refrigerator, I would have told her no, because she can't afford it.

"But God told me to buy it," she said.

"The blessings of the Lord have no sorrow attached," I answered, paraphrasing Proverbs 10:22. "I'm sure you wanted it, I'm sure you felt you needed it, but you could not afford it."

"Yes, I *can* afford it!" she insisted. "But now I need money to get through the month. What are you going to do about that?"

Well, I probably don't have to tell you that, in the words of my Texas brethren, I didn't do a darn tootin' thing about it. She messed up and bought something she had no business buying, and tantrum or not, it wasn't my job to fix it.

Cliff jumping is a funny and painful thing. It's a thrilling ride on the way down, but once you hit the bottom, you're usually too banged up to patch your own wounds, so you start calling for others to come scrape you up off the pavement. What's worse, cliff jumping and entitlement go hand in hand. Wounded cliff jumpers are demanding and quick to fashion a megaphone out of the God stick. It's hard to stay friends with cliff jumpers because they're always ordering everyone around them to clean up their messes and patch their wounds. And woe to you if you have a cliff jumper in your immediate family. You can sacrifice your entire life picking up their pieces.

They're also hard to help and very difficult to pastor. They tend to stick with their behavior patterns their entire lives because they never open up to the possibility that they might be doing something wrong.

Cliff jumping is easy to spot—in others. But how do we diagnose this behavior in ourselves?

Here are some primary clues.

1. Defensiveness: Do you get angry or defensive when friends start questioning your decisions?
2. A history of cliff jumping: Do most or all of your major life changes go badly? Do you always depend on the stars lining up perfectly in order to be successful? Are you always going out on a limb regardless of what's at stake? Is your life in a constant state of drama?
3. Telltale "mirrors": Do you get something along the lines of "Here we go again!" from people when you're making a big decision? Are you often dependent on others to recover from "setbacks"? Have you lost or damaged important relationships over major life changes? Have people told you they've had enough of your crises? The reactions of others often serve as an excellent mirror reflecting the true wisdom of our decisions.
4. A cliff jumper's attitude: Do you think that planning ahead is for chumps, regardless of the circumstances? Do you mock others for exercising caution? Do you always ignore due diligence for the thrill of flying by the seat of your pants?

Did some of those look familiar? Are you feeling a little uncomfortable right now? That's okay! The most important step in making a change is recognizing the need for change in the first place.

So how do you put a stop to the cliff-jumping behavior? Actually, it's not that hard.

1. Listen. Really listen to the people who care about you and give you input without selfish motivation. If you don't have friends like that, find some new friends. Notice I say *friends* here much more than family because, like it or not, and for better or for worse, advice from relatives usually comes fully loaded with a lifetime's worth of emotional baggage, ulterior motives, and personal agendas. God bless them for it, but maybe they love you so much they just don't want things to change. And you know what they say about the apple not falling far from the tree: you may be the product of a long line of banged-up cliff jumpers!

2. Make sure you have a safety net or a parachute, such as sufficient savings to sustain you if you don't earn any money for a while, or another job to keep the paychecks coming. Your income is your parachute. Savings are your safety net. Yes, God is our provider. But since manna doesn't rain down from heaven every morning, as it did when the Israelites were in the desert, most of us get our divine provision every two weeks via direct deposit. Don't squander that. That means *do not quit the job you have until you have found another one.*

3. Quitting without a plan while insisting that God will provide will not likely yield good results. Every once in a great while there is someone whose path involves quitting without another job in place, but there are usually other safety provisions in position, like a healthy emergency fund and confirmation from others who know there is something better for you just around the corner. No safety gear, no jump.

Same thing goes for any other major life decision: moving to a new state without a job once you get there. Getting married or getting divorced. Making major financial commitments. There's a time to be flippant about a choice. That time is when you are ordering a latte. Don't take lightly any decision with potentially heavy consequences.

4. Make sure you are moving toward something, not away from something. Making a big life leap just to get away from a bad situation is not the way to go. Unless you are suffering domestic abuse, violence, or other injustice, make sure you are moving toward the life you want and not taking a cliff jump away from your problems. The view can be pretty sweet at the top of the mountain, if a little cloudy. Yet the rocks below can be brutal. And if you jump before you deal with the problems, you will more than likely just take them with you.

5. Ask God for confirmation. That doesn't have to mean an audible voice from heaven, a burning bush, or a weird prophetic encounter from some babbling guy with a beard. But in my experience when you ask God for confirmation, He delivers. And in my experience, confirmation dribbles in with a steady, consistent pattern, and not necessarily a lightning bolt of "Yes!" or "No!" For example, you may find that all your friends and rational family members are on board. A collective agreement among the people in your life is one source of confirmation. A nod from one nutty friend is not the voice of God telling you to go forth. And collective agreement is *one* source of confirmation. Not all of it.

You may also stumble upon a passage of Scripture that you see in a fresh new way that seems to encourage the path you're considering. You may get an unexpected gift of a book related to your decision. You'll sleep well. There will be peace in your heart and calmness in your stomach. In drips and drabs the layers of confirmation will come, letting you know that it's safe to start moving ahead.

What if you're not a cliff jumper, but someone you love is? That's a difficult and often sticky place to be, but you don't have to hold yourself hostage to someone else's behavior. You will definitely want to reread the chapter on enabling, but for our discussion here it is critical that you understand that no one can make you own their problems. You have to sign up for that all by yourself.

Here's a tool that will help you and the cliff jumper in your life: coach him into "trying on" a decision to see how it fits before he moves forward.

It's like going to the Gap for a pair of jeans: because there are many different fits, colors, and styles, and therefore, different outcomes in how those jeans will look and feel once on, you have to grab your size in several different versions to find the one for you.

A major life decision can have as many different outcomes as the Gap has jeans. Try on your decision by taking baby steps toward it and seeing how well your decision "fits." It is much easier to take a step or two, then decide to turn around, than to go all the way and do something you can't take back.

If you have a cliff jumper in your life, you'll need to coach that individual over and over again to take a baby step, then stop, look, and listen to see if a train is coming before he or she takes the next step. If you come to that person's rescue time and time again, all you are doing is encouraging his or her recklessness and setting yourself up as the person expected to be at the bottom with the broom. Not fun.

The cumulative effect of a lifetime or even a few years of cliff jumping is not pretty: staggering debt, foreclosures, unpaid personal loans, and broken relationships are the norm. It takes a while to recover from such significant financial crises, and the fact that they were self-induced makes it a particularly painful process. But it's very possible to break this pattern, and unless you want to be broke and alone for the rest of your life, break it you must.

Stop Jumping Once and for All

I think one of the most powerful tools for cliff jumpers is accountability. Make yourself accountable to two or three people whose judgment you trust, people who will always have your best interests at heart. Ask them to hold you accountable to them for making good decisions and ensuring your safety gear is in place before you jump. If they throw up red flags, stop in your tracks and thank them for loving you enough to keep you from sabotaging yourself once again.

And the next time you're making a big decision, make a list of all the consequences you face if the choice you're making is the wrong one. No job in place? What happens when you have no income for several months? And for each consequence, you must list an action plan to deal with it. If any part of your action plan involves calling on someone else to bail you out, that's a red flag that you're stepping off the cliff. Once it's all on paper, either you'll be confirmed that you are doing the right thing, you will decide to wait until the smoke clears, or you will scrap your plans for a safer path altogether. Either way, you'll have peace, and you will take giant leaps toward ensuring your life is never in shambles again.

Another reason to put this bad habit behind you is that in doing so, you will make it much easier to maintain a healthy level of faith.

Think about it this way: if you've been in the habit of doing crazy stuff because "God told you to," it's got to mess with your head and your heart when things don't work out well. That gets you to wondering why God let you down, when the truth is, God never, ever lets us down. We stumble only when we go our own way.

This line of thought is why so many people I coach think their problems are all God's fault. It's crazy, mixed-up thinking, but it makes perfect sense to someone who thinks God told him or her to do it.

Taking responsibility for your decisions takes a healthy dose of maturity, but once you do, you'll sleep better at night. You can trust that the Holy Spirit will guide you to make the right decisions instead of wondering why God let you down.

A prayer for cliff jumpers:

Heavenly Father, I need Your help, Your guidance, and Your wisdom. I have a pattern of making bad decisions and thinking I'm doing something that You wanted me to do. Please help me understand the difference between Your will and my will. Surround me with wise friends who will help me see when I am about to make a mistake. Give me a spirit of discernment and boldness tempered with an understanding that bold leaps of faith require waiting on You for confirmation, blessing, and guidance. Thank You, Father, for being able to turn even my mistakes into something glorious that will bless my family and me. I surrender my life and all of my circumstances to You.

In Jesus' name I pray, amen.

God's Way

Here are the most important points to take away from chapter 8.

- Taking crazy risks does not mean you have great faith; it just means you like to jump off cliffs without a parachute. Not smart.
- Confirmation is the difference between following an impulse and answering a divine calling.
- Heeding the wisdom of the smart people around you is like a safety net in case you get too close to the edge. Listen to wisdom and you will bounce right back.
- We *cannot* put God's name on our impulses. Sometimes God does call us to take bold leaps. But you have to have the maturity and discernment to know when something is God and when it's just your impulses flaring up.

- To ascribe God's name to the chaotic fallout of a personal choice goes against the very nature of who we know God to be.
- The Holy Spirit gives us a good gauge by which to judge when we're about to do something foolish: inner peace. No peace, no jump.
- Be wary of the "God told me to" declaration. People who use the "God stick" usually do so to bully someone else into supporting their bad decision.
- When making a major, life-changing decision, consider carefully the advice of friends and others who have your best interests at heart.
- Don't quit your job until you have lined up another one.
- Always make sure that life changes are moving you toward something, not away from something. You cannot run away from your problems.
- Ask God for confirmation that you're making the right decision.
- Help cliff jumpers "try on" a decision before they leap.

Solution Steps

Here are simple steps you can take today to help you and your family look before you leap:

1. Learn the difference between risk and faith, and never equate one with the other. If God wants you to take a big leap, pray hard before you jump, and get confirmation in the form of counsel from friends, your pastor, and others who want the very best for you.
2. If you're weighing a major life change, make a list of factors pointing to "yes" and factors pointing to "no." There will always be at least a few entries in both columns, but one will stand out in time as the clear winner.

3. Determine once and for all—and write it down—that you will never again rush into a major decision. God is never in a hurry, and you don't have to be either.

4. Begin using your inner peace and the soundness of your sleep as a gauge to determine if you're on the right path.

5. Try on decisions before you make them. Decide in your mind what you are going to do and see how the decision feels before you actually act on it.

6. Pray, pray, and pray some more. Ask for wisdom and confirmation. God will give it to you, every time.

7. Make a commitment to yourself that from now on, you won't blame God when things don't go as planned. If you make a mistake, own it. God has promised that his plans for us are to prosper us and not to harm us (Jer. 29:11). God will never throw us off the cliff, but we certainly have the free will to jump.

8. Forbid yourself to say, "God told me to" for every decision you make.

9. While cliff jumping is easy to spot in others, it is really hard to diagnose this condition in our own hearts. If you suspect that you might be a cliff jumper, ask yourself these questions:

- Do I get angry or defensive when friends start questioning my decisions?
- Do most or all of my major life changes go badly? Is my life in a constant state of drama?
- Do I hear, 'Here we go again!' from people when I'm making a big decision? Am I often dependent on others to recover from 'setbacks'? (Others' reactions often serve as an excellent mirror reflecting the true wisdom of our decisions.)
- Do I tend to think that planning ahead is for chumps, regardless of the circumstances? Do I mock others for

exercising caution? Do I consistently ignore due diligence for the thrill of flying by the seat of my pants?

Some of these steps can't be taken without some very real effort. But if you will put forth that effort, they will pay great dividends—in the form of *financial freedom!*

NINE

THE CONVICTION CLEAN-UP PLAN

Okay, you've done the hard part.

You've rooted through your counterfeit convictions and cleaned some of the junk out of your heart. You should have some understanding of not only why you've done some of the stupid things you've done with your money but also how to apply biblical truths to future behavior to break those bad habits of the past.

But it's not quite time to ride off into the sunset, is it? Now that you're no longer doing the dumb stuff, time to do some smart stuff, like putting together a spending plan that reflects your new, healthier habits.

In chapter 6, I showed you an ideal spending formula of 10-10-80: 10 percent giving, 10 percent savings, and 80 percent living expenses. Because our God is a God of grace and He allows us time to heal past wounds and recover from past mistakes, my spending plans do as well.

Before diving in, however, there are a couple of important points to consider:

1. Budgets are never "done." Just as your laundry hamper doesn't stay empty for long, neither does your budget stay "done" after one time. A budget is an organic, living thing that reflects your financial picture at any given time. Because your life changes all the time, your spending plan must change accordingly.

2. Creating a spending plan should not be tedious. Don't get me wrong—if you love spending four hours each month creating a mammoth spreadsheet that details everything from your mortgage payment to gummy bear expenses, knock yourself out. But that's not the way I do it, and it's not the way you have to do it either. Your spending plan should take fifteen minutes or so, tops. Just write out your plan, and be done with it. There's laundry to do, after all.

3. Your spending plan should be personal. It should reflect you, your goals, your circumstances, and your actual expenses. The forms here are a guideline: use them to create something that makes sense to you.

4. Be realistic. Don't try to create the "perfect" average-month budget that doesn't take into consideration the fact that your daughter's birthday is the fourteenth and the dog is due for a teeth cleaning. If you know the expense is coming, plan for it. At least you'll know exactly what you are dealing with.

5. Make it pretty. Don't discount the value of aesthetics when doing something as potentially tedious as budgeting. Once a year, I go out and buy the prettiest binder I can find in which to keep my monthly bills and budgets. You've got to look at the thing all the time; why not make it attractive?

My budgeting system includes three different levels for three different financial positions. We're all at different places in our lives and in our money, and I personally think one-size-fits-all budgeting systems are a recipe for frustration.

Level One is for people who are still struggling through credit card, student loan, and auto loan debt. Here you'll reduce expenses to get outgo below income, begin giving and saving, and gradually reduce living expenses over time until you get them to a point where you have a workable budget.

Level Two is where you live out the 10-10-80 plan and take it to the next level by paying off your mortgage and making sure your spending accurately reflects your priorities and values. Here I assume you've eliminated all debts except your mortgage, and therefore we can really examine lifestyle choices and spending allotments so you can make sure your spending lines up with your goals and values.

Level Three is the fun part! Here is where you develop a spending plan based on the assumptions that you own your home and cars debt free, and that you are now at liberty to structure your income in a way that allows you to focus on your giving and investment goals.

Most people hate "budgeting." I certainly do, but I love working on my monthly "wealth allocation plan." Whether you have $300 or $300 million, that's wealth, and you need to allocate it. Doesn't that sound like more fun than "budgeting"? I also don't mind planning for the future, when that future includes putting my three boys through college and having the occasional nice beach vacation with my family.

Even if you don't like crunching numbers, take the time to understand the ideal spending allocations I've assigned to these different categories. Understanding a percentage range that you expect to spend in a particular category will make it easier for you to make wise decisions when the opportunity arises to make a change. For example, if you take a job in a new city, you'll need to find a home. Knowing that you should select a home with payments that fall below a certain percentage of your income will help you make a wise choice for the long haul.

And again, not all of these ideas can be implemented tomorrow, but they can get you thinking about ways you can implement meaningful change today. Little changes here and there, compounded over time, will cause dramatic changes in your financial picture more quickly than you ever thought possible.

And even though you may not be at Level Three yet, I want you to walk through that spending plan regardless of your current circumstances. Writing down what you think your Level Three life could look like will encourage you to keep going on your financial journey. Here's why: having goals written down on paper with a set of actionable steps to achieve them makes them attainable goals and not lofty, pie-in-the-sky dreams.

Do you want to be one of those people who simply dreams about owning a beach house, or do you want to have the keys in your hands?

Do you want to talk about opening a vaccine clinic in Nicaragua, or do you want to be there to turn the first shovelful of dirt?

Do you want to talk about how nice it would be to have the life you have always dreamed of, or do you want to *have* it?

Writing down what you want and a clear path to get there will create the space in your life that you need to eliminate stress, hear God more clearly, and move toward the dreams He has put in your heart. But you have to know that your dreams are attainable, and that requires writing them down and coming up with a plan to achieve them.

Henry Ford put it this way: "If you think you can do a thing or think you can't do a thing, you're right."

What a difference a plan makes.

Level One

In Level One, your focus needs to be on stabilizing and minimizing your expenses so you can put the maximum amount possible toward paying off debt.

If you're not already giving regularly to your local church, this plan will allow you to start gradually, eventually working your way up to a

10 percent tithe. It will also allow you to begin saving, which is absolutely critical for your long-term financial health.

The first step to creating a Level One spending plan is to know exactly what you are spending for everything in your life. You can't just guess. You must have a realistic picture based on actual spending in order to properly manage where your money goes. This means you'll have to track your spending for at least a month, ideally for three months. Since you may not have veterinarian and dentist bills, carpet cleaning, and insurance premiums due every month, you need to track what's going out for at least three months so you're catching all the outgo.

In the meantime, work off a simple budget you create based on existing assumptions about what you're spending. As you go through your first three months, make a lot of notes about which categories you guessed correctly for and which categories need more or less money allocated for them.

One of the goals of Level One is to find any areas where money is being wasted. This doesn't mean you're a bad person if you go to the movies and out to dinner with your sweetie once a month, if that is something you value and you have planned for it. However, you may find you're spending $200 a month on movies, and because your list of life goals does not include becoming a movie critic, you may decide to reduce spending on entertainment at this point in your financial life. It's your money and your call. So try to look at your spending without judging or condemning yourself too much. The goal here is merely to get an accurate picture of what you're spending. Then you can judge and condemn yourself later, once you know what you're really shelling out each month. (Just kidding, of course.)

Once you know what you're spending, you can lump your budget items into general categories such as the following:

Giving: Tithes to your church and charitable contributions to any organizations.

Savings: Money put into savings or retirement accounts.

Housing: Mortgage or rent payment, utilities, maintenance, insurance, taxes, household needs (stamps, cleaning supplies, toilet paper, gas for the mower, and so forth).

Food: Groceries, snacks away from the house, restaurant meals, kids' lunches, etc.

Transportation: Car payments, repairs, gas and oil, insurance, speeding tickets (I actually had this as a budget category for a while when we lived in Texas. Those Fort Worth police are vicious!). And yes, car payments are debt, and they should be paid off as quickly as possible as soon as your credit card debts are paid off. However, for the purposes of the Level One budget, include them in the transportation category.

Clothing: Clothing. Need I say more? Clothes and shoes for the kids and yourselves. Band and karate uniforms. Sweaters for the dog.

Entertainment: Cable or satellite TV bill (this does *not* go under housing!), Internet and cell phone (unless required for work, in which case you can count them as work expenses; no cheating, though), movies, subscriptions, kids' activities, and so forth.

Personal care: Haircuts, toiletries, manicures, tanning salon, Botox.

Insurance and medical: Life insurance, disability, medical—premiums for every kind of insurance you have except home and car go into this category. If you have health-related expenses, such as medications, doctor visits, and other needs, they should go into this category as well.

Other: School tuition, pet care, allowances, and "blow money." Keep this category small; otherwise it will turn into something resembling your kitchen junk drawer overnight, and you'll be back to wondering why you're missing $800 a month.

Debts: Someday this category will disappear. Until that day comes, manage your debt aggressively, and pay it off as soon as you can. That's easier said than done, of course, so here are some quick tips that will help you pay down debt as quickly as possible.

- **Prioritize.** Figure out which debts are eating your lunch the most. These are the ones with the highest interest rates, ridiculous fees, and other "extras" that make them particularly difficult to pay down. Or they could be personal debts that are bothering you because they are affecting the relationship. Or perhaps you have a student loan debt that you would like to pay off. If it's a credit card you wish to focus on, contact your creditors and ask for an interest rate reduction. If they won't lower your rate, threaten to take your business to another credit card. Usually this tactic works, although you may have to try several times. Be persistent and polite and don't give up. Focus your first efforts on the cards with the highest rates, but work on getting all your interest rates as low as possible. After you've done that, aim to pay them off in the order of highest balance: target the lowest balance first, and work your way up the ladder.

- **Stop charging.** You cannot dig your way out of a hole. Cut up your credit cards, or better yet, run them through the shredder. For some reason, shredding is more gratifying. If you're carrying debt from month to month and trying to get out of the credit card cycle, carrying plastic in your wallet is like being an alcoholic and showing up to an AA meeting with a flask in your hand. Don't be that person. And don't close the accounts unless you have a wonderfully low interest rate that you would

> **You cannot dig your way out of a hole.**

like to lock in. Once you close an account (which, by the way, you can do even if you have an outstanding balance), you cannot change the terms, such as requesting a lower interest rate. Once the account is closed, the terms remain in place until the balance is paid in full, unless, of course, you default on the account by failing to make payments. Then things get ugly.

- **Pay more than the minimum:** If you're only making the minimum payments on your cards, you very well could stay in debt until you die, and that is no exaggeration. You have to pay more than the minimums. In the Level One budget, I recommend paying the minimums *plus* an additional 10 percent of your take-home pay toward the debt with the lowest balance. Once that account is paid in full, take the full amount you were paying toward the first debt (minimum plus 10 percent of your take-home pay) toward the second debt.

  And to answer your question, yes, it is hard to free up an additional 10 percent of your income to put toward debts. You may think you can't do it, but I bet with hard work and sacrifice (cable? manicures?) you can do it. There is *always* room to cut.

- **If you can't pay all your bills,** you need to get some help managing your budget and finding ways to cut expenses. I recommend Financial Peace University. You can find a class near you at www.daveramsey.com. In the meantime, you must come up with a budget in which your outgo is less than your income. Make cuts where you can, and take care of life's necessities first: food, clothing (only if absolutely needed), housing, transportation, and child care, if that is necessary in order for you to work. Your next priority is your debts. Try to make at least the minimum payments. If you can't even do that, you must call your creditors and explain your situation. *Everything else in your budget is nego-tiable*, and I do mean everything. Cell phones, cable TV, gym memberships, everything else can go. It's only tempo-rary. You can do it.

But take care of your family's basic needs first. It is not okay to make your credit card payments but not your mort-gage payment, or not have money for groceries. You need food and shelter to live. Visa will not shrivel up and die if you make a late payment or a partial payment during this process. Again, it is only temporary.

And by the same token, it is not okay to have a $200 cell phone bill and not be paying on your credit cards. Remember Psalm 37:21 says: "The wicked borrows and does not repay." If you have cut everything out of your budget and still can't cover all your debts, you need to work something out with your creditors. You've made some mistakes, but you're not a bad person. But if you're ignoring your debts while keeping your little luxuries, that's not okay. Do the honorable thing and sacrifice what you have to in order to pay your debts.

Now that you have the basic budgeting concepts down, here's a sample budget form, including percentages I recommend for differ-ent categories. These are recommended categories just to give you an idea of what I consider healthy and reasonable for different areas. If you live in New York or San Francisco, for example, you may spend significantly more on housing than what I listed here, but you can compensate for that by reducing spending in other areas. Another sig-nificant change you may see in your own budget is that the less you earn and the larger your family, the greater percentage of your budget you will need to allocate toward food. If you make less than $30,000 a year and you have two children, you could reasonably expect to spend 20 percent or more of your budget on food. That's okay, as long as it is realistic and you can balance your budget. The only real rule is that your spending percentages must add up to 100 percent. You must account for every dollar.

Category	Recommended Percentage	Budgeted Amount	Actual Amount	Actual Percentage
Giving	10%			
Savings	10%			
Housing	30%			
Food	8%			
Transportation	10%			
Clothing	5%			
Child care	[5% (must come from other area)]			
Debts	15%			
Personal care	2%			
Insurance/ medical	5%			
Entertainment	4%			
Other	1%			

Let's examine what an actual Level One budget might look like for a hypothetical family. Ron and Margie Abbott both work, and they bring home $6,500 a month combined. They do not have child care expenses, but they do have $12,000 in outstanding credit card debts. The minimum payment on those debts is $325 a month. They have one car payment of $247 a month. Here's what their budgeted amounts would look like:

Category	Recommended Percentage	Budgeted Amount	Actual Amount	Actual Percentage
Giving	10%	$650		
Savings	10%	$650		
Housing	30%	$1,950		
Food	8%	$520		
Transportation	10%	$650		
Clothing	5%	$325		
Child care	[5% (must come from other area)]	$0		
Debts	15%	$975		
Personal care	2%	$130		
Insurance/ medical	5%	$325		
Entertainment	4%	$260		
Other	1%	$65		

That's a decent start for Ron and Margie, but they have some changes they would like to make. First of all, their mortgage payment is $1,700 a month, including taxes and insurance. But utilities run an average of $300 a month, and they really need to be saving $150 a month to replace their furnace.

Also, because their car payment is $247 and they live near both their offices, their total transportation costs are only about $375 a month. They think they can spend less than the recommended percentages on personal care and entertainment and do not anticipate clothing needs in the near future. However, their out-of-pocket health insurance costs are $300 a month; plus, they have life insurance premiums due once a year that have an average monthly cost of $125. And Ron takes a daily medication that costs $55 a month. They would like to be more aggressive with their debt payoff. So with those revisions, here's what Ron and Margie's budget might look like:

Category	Recommended Percentage	Budgeted Amount	Actual Amount	Actual Percentage *Rounded
Giving	10%	$650	$650	10%
Savings	10%	$650	$650	10%
Housing	30%	$1,950	$2150	33%
Food	8%	$520	$520	8%
Transportation	10%	$650	$375	5%
Clothing	5%	$325	$0	0%
Child care	[5% (must come from other area)]	$0	$0	0%
Debts	15%	$975	$1,400	22%
Personal care	2%	$130	$100	2%
Insurance/ medical	5%	$325	$480	7%
Entertainment	4%	$260	$110	2%
Other	1%	$65	$65	1%

Is their budget "bad" because they don't follow the percentages exactly? Of course not! No one has an "average" life that lines up perfectly on a chart. The trick is creating a chart that lines up with your life. The budget serves you, not the other way around. Ron and Margie's budget reflects their values, doesn't exceed their income, and allows for giving and savings. It's a great Level One budget.

Let's look at another hypothetical Level One family, one whose finances don't line up so neatly as Ron and Margie's.

Paula Guthridge is a divorced, single mother of three. Her monthly income is $2,300, and her current monthly outgo is $2,500. She is supposed to be getting an additional $1,600 a month in child support from her ex-husband, but he has not paid in three months. The budget she's been working from lists her income as $3,900 a month, which is why she's overspending. Paula relies on credit cards to pay for groceries and other incidentals when she doesn't get child support. She has an outstanding credit card balance of $1,900 and a monthly car payment of $325. She got the car and the house in the divorce settlement, but she also got the payments attached.

> No one has an "average" life that lines up perfectly on a chart.

She's not giving or saving. Her ex-husband is responsible for the kids' health insurance and medical expenses, so she only has to cover her own. She has no life insurance, and her only indulgences are a $30 monthly pedicure and taking the kids out for dinner and a movie once a month. She hits the ATM once a week and takes out $100 in cash. That money pays for fast-food trips; incidentals; and money the kids need for school projects, activities, field trips, and more.

Her current recommended budget spending compared to her actual spending looks like this:

Category	Recommended Percentage	Budgeted Amount	Actual Amount	Actual Percentage
Giving	10%	$230	$0	0%
Savings	10%	$230	$0	0%
Housing	30%	$690	$1,100	48%
Food	8%	$184	$600	26%
Transportation	10%	$230	$400	17%

Clothing	5%	$115	$85	4%
Child care	5%	$115	$600	26%
Debts	10%	$230	$75	3%
Personal care	2%	$46	$60	3%
Insurance/ medical	5%	$115	$150	7%
Entertainment	4%	$92	$75	3%
Other	1%	$23	$400	17%
Total	100%	$2,300	$3,545	154%

Paula is spending 54 percent more than she earns every month. And she's not setting aside anything for future needs. Paula's budget is a train wreck, and she wasn't realizing it because she was planning her life based on $3,900 a month. This is a common problem for single parents. You *must* budget according to the income you know you can count on. If your ex has been late on a child support payment or failed to pay altogether *even once*, you must establish a baseline budget based only on *your* income. Then you can have a list of other expenses to cover if and when the child support money comes in.

Also, Paula's mortgage payment is too high for her single-mom income. While it will take time to sell the home and find something less expensive, it is a worthwhile thing to consider. Same thing with her car. She cannot afford that much of a car payment. We can't budget around that right away, but we can help Paula trim other expenses by encouraging her to use coupons and cut out the little luxuries and ATM withdrawals. If Paula really got serious with grocery coupons, she could cut her food spending by half. Paula also must get life insurance to protect her children. Because she is relatively young and healthy, she could switch to a less expensive health-care plan at work and save on her out-of-pocket medical insurance costs.

Another significant savings: because her children are school age, if she could hire a neighborhood teen to watch them after school instead of paying for a pricier day care, she could significantly trim her child care expenses.

Here's what Paula's initial revised budget looks like:

Category	Recommended Percentage	Budgeted Amount	Actual Amount	Actual Percentage
Giving	10%	$230	$23	1%
Savings	10%	$230	$23	1%
Housing	30%	$690	$1,100	48%
Food	8%	$184	$300	13%
Transportation	10%	$230	$391	17%
Clothing	5%	$115	$0	0%
Child care	5%	$115	$300	13%
Debts	10%	$230	$69	3%
Personal Care	2%	$46	$25	1%
Insurance/ Medical	5%	$115	$69	3%
Entertainment	4%	$92	$0	0%
Other	1%	$23	$0	0%
Total	100%	$2,300	$2,300	100%

This budget doesn't include everything Paula wants, but it ensures that she can survive those months when she doesn't receive child support without resorting to credit cards.

At this point Paula is owed $4,800 in back child support. If she gets that, I would advise her to pay off the credit card and put the

> Single parents have to be unwavering in their dedication to creating a workable spending plan and then sticking to it.

rest into savings for emergencies. Any future child support payments should go toward paying off the car to eliminate the car payment. If the back child support is paid and her ex starts paying again, she could keep her home if she watches her spending in other categories.

Single parents have to be unwavering in their dedication to creating a workable spending plan and then sticking to it. When it's all up to you, there is no room for error.

Level Two

You've got to love Level Two. All the debt is gone except for the mortgage. You can take a vacation and pay cash for it without worrying about whether you will still be able to pay the mortgage as well. I recommend that in Level Two you take the 10 percent of your take-home pay that you were putting toward your debts and direct it toward paying off your mortgage as quickly as possible.

The only times when mortgage payoff might be less attractive are when your job is in jeopardy or if you know you don't intend to stay in your home for the long term.

If you are at all at risk of unemployment, it is imperative that you put away as much cash as possible to sustain you if you do indeed lose your job. Even if you *think* your job is secure, an emergency fund is a must. How big your emergency fund needs to be depends on your income, your current expenses, and how long you can reasonably expect to be out of work. (What's reasonable? Ask someone with a job like yours who has been through unemployment how long it took to find work; then double that time frame. At a minimum, aim for six months' basic living expenses.)

Also, if you don't expect to stay in your home, you might be better off stashing extra cash into savings rather than paying down the mortgage. Or you can split the difference: I often counsel people who are stuck on whether to save or pay down debt to split the difference, or to take the extra cash and put half toward savings and half toward debt.

The bottom line is that no one has a life that fits perfectly into budgeting categories. Generally speaking, though, choose the conservative route, and the path that helps you save more and pay down debt more quickly.

I've eliminated the debt category and added the mortgage payoff acceleration category. I have kept them separate because in the event of an emergency, you could direct those funds toward medical bills, car repairs, or whatever else comes up. I've also increased the savings category to 20 percent. You need an emergency fund of at least six months of living expenses in an easily accessible account. After that you must start maxing out your retirement savings.

Transportation costs dwindle to almost nothing when you own your cars debt free. I've also increased the entertainment budget. It's time to have some fun after all your hard work becoming debt free!

Category	Recommended Percentage
Giving	10%
Savings	20%
Housing	30%
Mortgage payoff	10%
Food	8%
Transportation	3%
Clothing	5%
Personal care	2%
Insurance / medical	5%
Entertainment	6%
Other	1%

Let's see how Ron and Margie's budget might look at Level Two. Let's assume that they still have the same income and they have paid off their credit card debts and their car and finally got that furnace replaced, but that all other expenses remain the same. The only change they would like to make is that in addition to tithing to their local church, they would like to start donating $150 a month to an international charity that helps children in extreme poverty, and Ron and Margie don't need as much money for clothing.

Here's how their budget would look:

Category	Recommended Percentage	Budgeted Amount	Actual Percentage
Giving	10%	$800	12%
Savings	20%	$1,300	20%
Housing	30%	$2,000	31%
Mortgage payoff	10%	$650	10%
Food	8%	$520	8%
Transportation	3%	$195	3%
Clothing	5%	$125	2%
Personal care	2%	$130	2%
Insurance / medical	5%	$325	5%
Entertainment	6%	$390	6%
Other	1%	$65	1%

This is a spending plan that would bring joy to any middle-class American household, and it's perfectly attainable: it might not happen overnight, but if you work hard, eliminate your counterfeit convictions, and spend and plan wisely, it can happen for you, too, likely sooner than you think.

Level Three

Imagine a life with no debt. If you stick with the Level Two budget and persevere in paying down your mortgage with at least an additional 10 percent of your income, you can likely pay off your mortgage in five years or fewer, depending, of course, on how much you owe and your income.

But if it takes seven years or even ten, you're on a significantly faster track to debt-free home ownership than most Americans, many of whom will never get to own their homes free and clear. Imagine how much fun it would be to owe nothing to anyone! No house payments, no car payments, nothing but taxes and utilities and food and other daily needs and expenses. What in the world would you do with all that extra money?

In Level Three, you get to decide *exactly* what you would do with all that money. The options are endless, and quite fun to consider.

When Ron and Margie hit Level Three, housing costs are reduced to taxes and insurance, about $300 a month. That frees them up to give more, save more, and have a lot more fun! Here the percentages become less important. What really matters is that you continue to save for future needs, give to bless others, and let your spending reflect your goals and values. Ron and Margie decided that when they hit Level Three, they want to really start investing and also saving to pay cash for a really nice car.

Category	Recommended Percentage	Budgeted Amount
Giving	20%	$1,300
Savings	30%	$1,950
Housing	5%	$325
Food	8%	$520
Transportation	14%	$910

Clothing	5%	$325
Personal care	2%	$130
Insurance / medical	5%	$325
Entertainment	10%	$650
Other	1%	$65

Ron and Margie will become very wealthy very quickly under this plan. If they invest $1,950 a month at an average rate of return of 8 percent, they would be millionaires in nineteen years. That's not a long time in the whole scheme of things, especially considering most Americans live their entire lives never achieving the million-dollar wealth mark.

Living Out Your Plan

I've outlined here some suggestions on how to make a budget that works, but the key is developing a spending plan that works for *you*. Like a nimble boxer in the ring, your spending plan should bob and weave and duck when needed, in response to any sucker punches life may throw at you in any given month. It should reflect your personality, your comfort level with risk, and your life as you actually live it.

> **The key is developing a spending plan that works for *you*.**

If your budget is so complicated that it takes an hour to figure out how to move money around to cover an unexpected tire replacement without dipping into savings, your budget is too complicated. Conversely, if you don't know what you're spending in restaurants compared to the grocery store, it may be too simple. You have to find what's right for you. But hitting your stride in your spending plan is a lot like hitting your stride anywhere else in life: when it's right, you just know.

And what's right for you may not be right for someone else, but that's okay. Generally speaking, though, here are three characteristics that every good budget should have:

1. It should be current. Most of the budgets people bring to me are flawed because they simply don't accurately reflect the family's current income and expenses. Sometimes the income is off because they haven't revised their budget in two years, and they've gotten raises since then. Or the budget amount for cell phones doesn't include the fact that one of their children recently got a cell phone, adding an additional monthly charge for the extra line and unlimited texting to their plan. When you make a budget, make sure it reflects your life today.

2. It should be inclusive. If you have six cats and three dogs, you better have budget categories for the veterinarian and for pet food. If for the past four years you have not been able to ignore the siren call of the beach come Memorial Day weekend, by all means, start saving for that getaway in January.

3. It should be realistic. Some of us have tough financial realities we have to face every month. Refusing to budget for them does not make the problems go away, but it *will* add new problems to the list. For example, most single parents I counsel include child support as part of their income whether they receive child support or not. And many small business owners who ask for my help aren't setting money aside for their quarterly tax bills, causing needless panic four times a year. Don't ignore your reality. It will catch up with you eventually whether you plan for it or not, so you might as well plan for it.

If there is ever a good time to pray, I think it's right before you write your spending plan for the month. I always pray before I do our

If there is ever a good time to pray, it's right before you write your spending plan for the month.

monthly budget; then Scott and I go over it together, and we pray over it again. If you believe that God owns it all and we're entrusted with a portion to use wisely, it's good to continually ask for wisdom, discernment, patience, and God's blessings on the decisions you make regarding your money.

Here's a prayer that will help you ask God for His blessings on your finances:

Dear God, thank You for everything You have provided to us, our incomes, home, food, clothing, and all the little things that bless us every day. Give us wisdom in the choices we make regarding the money with which You have blessed us. Let our choices honor You, bless our family, and enable us to help others. Help us have open hearts to give to others, the discipline to save, and the discernment to live below our means on what is left over. Help us stretch our dollars so that we can get more for what we spend. Please help us find ways to save money so that every dollar goes farther. Help us to be content with what we have so we don't needlessly want for things we don't really need. Let our financial decisions reflect our values and our priorities. Protect us from outside influences that promote greed, discontent, and wastefulness. Heavenly Father, we know all good things come from You, so please help us make the most of every blessing You give to us.

In Jesus' name I pray, amen.

CONCLUSION

Your Money God's Way

Our God is the Author and Creator of order and peace. It is not God's will for any of His children to live in chaos, frustration, lack, and debt. When we take responsibility for our thoughts, feelings, actions, and attitudes, we allow God into our lives and our finances, and we give Him room to bless us in the ways we have been praying for.

Money is just money. It's not who we are or who we are meant to be. Having more doesn't make us better people. Having less doesn't make us bad people. But broke believers are a lousy testimony to an awesome God. If we get our heads and hearts right, we can line ourselves up with what He is doing, and our lives will mirror what God wants for us, in us, and through us.

I sincerely hope this time has allowed you to heal some hurts from the past and to clear up some muddy thinking. I also hope you've given yourself permission to aggressively pursue the financial freedom that God designed for each of us. I hope you have learned to say no to yourself and to others and that you feel empowered and informed, so you can make your best possible plan to address your current financial picture, while also being free to dream big dreams for what's ahead.

I hope you understand the potential of the power of God that lies within you.

I know this journey is not easy. I've cried your tears and prayed your prayers. I've been humbled hundreds of times and have been brought to my knees before God daily. I've doubted, regained my faith, doubted again, then believed again. I have to believe that is a normal part of the human experience. As long as we get our faith back for another run, there's nothing we can't do through the power of God that lies within us.

The power of God is in you, with you, and all around you. He loves you, where you are, right now, imperfections and all. You are a perfect creation in His eyes. He wants to hear your prayers, bless you, keep you, and comfort you. He wants to walk with you and be your friend.

I hope every twist and turn of your financial journey is filled with miracles big and small. I hope your journey to financial freedom is shorter than you ever thought it could be and more fulfilling that you ever hoped for. I hope you get to a place where you can see that God has made your life better for having walked this road than if you had never walked it at all. That's the power of serving God. He takes your mess and makes it your message. That is what He has done for me, and it is what He will do for you, too. When you're well on your journey to financial freedom, I hope you'll pause and help others join you on that road. Financial burdens are misery. We have to help one another walk through them. Helping others is what makes the journey worthwhile.

> **The power of God is in you, with you, and all around you.**

I leave you with the blessing of 1 Corinthians 15:10. In this passage, understand that the author, the apostle Paul, had been a persecutor of Christians. It was on the road to Damascus that Paul met Jesus and gave his life to Christ.

Paul's baggage dwarfed anything, I'm sure, that you might feel you have between you and God. Yet if God cared enough to pursue Paul, He cares enough to pursue you too.

The verse reads, "By the grace of God I am what I am, and His grace toward me was not in vain; but I labored more abundantly than they all, yet not I, but the grace of God which was with me."

I pray you feel surrounded by God's grace every day and that you will "labor more abundantly" and get out of debt and be financially free faster than you ever thought possible. The grace of God is with you, raining down on you from heaven. And here on earth, I am cheering for you all the way.

A final prayer:

Father God, thank You for the love You have for me, right here and right now. Thank You for giving Your Son, Jesus, to die on the cross for all who have sinned, including me. I accept Your Son, Jesus Christ, as my Savior, and I ask that You forgive all of my sins and give me eternal life. God, please show me Your ways and how I can live a life that honors You. Help me to bless others, care for my family, and live the life that You designed for me. I love You, I trust You, and I put my life in Your hands.

In Jesus' name I pray, amen.

ACKNOWLEDGMENTS

I am so grateful to the many people who helped me get my passion onto paper.

My dear friends Lesley Conn and Richard Walters have stuck by my side for more years than any of us will admit to. "There is a friend who sticks closer than a brother," and I'm lucky to have you both. I'll be in my porch rocker with you guys. Thanks for putting up with me.

Deborah Mash has been a faithful mentor and friend. Her intelligence, strength, guidance, clear thinking, and constant words of encouragement and faith, not only in me but also in God's plans for me, have kept me going through moments of doubt. Deborah, I want to be you when I grow up.

Carol Trelstad is the big sister I always wanted. She is a prayer warrior, encourager, companion, and friend. If everyone had someone like Carol loving them and praying for them, the world would be a better place. Thank you, Carol, for your faithful prayers and support. I will be your little sister always.

Barry and Roxanne Nations, thank you for sharing your journey with me. A girl could not ask for better friends. Love you—mean it!

In a time when everyone is too busy, my friend and fellow author Peter Hirsch championed my idea and helped get me started. Thank you, Peter, that even in the midst of your own full life, you were not too busy to help an old friend.

My agent, David Hale Smith, invested a lot of time and energy in helping me share my message with the world. Thank you for believing in this idea and in me.

Melissa Brown, you not only gave me your friendship and loved my boys as if they were your own; you unknowingly started my journey to financial health when you bought those CDs. Thank you.

Jeff Drott, I am so glad God brought our paths together. You are a wonderful pastor, mentor, and friend. Thank you for your leadership, your listening ear, and your patience, friendship, and encouragement.

Jerry and Janet Patton, thank you for investing your time, prayers, and love in us, and for not passing out when we told you how much debt we had. We will forever be grateful to you for being our budget coaches when we first got started trying to dig out of our mess.

To my wonderful friends and partners in ministry at New Life Church: I couldn't do it without you. Joe and Menchie Littlefield, Dan and Amy Tyndale, Brent and Linda Ebaugh, Suzie Stoke, Chad and Leah Sahhar, Lindsey Mote, Mary Harms, Kevin Rohan, Steve and Erica Leafgreen, Alice Scott, and many others, thank you for your friendship, your laughter, and your faithful service to the great people of New Life. I love you all.

To my Gateway Church friends, especially Pam and Andy Beene, Jeff and Amy Duncan, and Pastors Linda Godsey and Alan Smith, thank you for your friendship as I transitioned from journalist to pastor. I'm sure it wasn't pretty, so thanks for ignoring my awkwardness and loving me through it.

I offer special thanks to Pastor Brady Boyd of New Life Church in Colorado Springs, Colorado, and Pastor Robert Morris of Gateway Church in Southlake, Texas. It takes a lot of guts to preach the tough, uncomfortable lessons, especially those about money, giving, and the condition of our hearts. Thank you for teaching the tough stuff. I am forever changed because of what I have learned from you.

And to the wonderful team at Thomas Nelson, I offer my deepest and most humble appreciation for all you've done to make this book a reality. Your team is amazing. Particular thanks to my editor, Bryan Norman, for taking my words and ideas and adding the polish of someone who truly understands how important it is that we Christians get this money stuff right.

This book is intended to provide accurate information with regard to the subject matter covered. However, the author and the publisher accept no responsibility for inaccuracies or omissions, and the author and publisher specifically disclaim any liability, loss, or risk, whether personal, financial, or otherwise, that is incurred as a consequence, directly or indirectly, from the use and/or application of any of the contents of this book.

This book is based, in part, on true events, but certain liberties have been taken with names, places, and dates, and the characters have been invented. Therefore, the persons and characters portrayed bear absolutely no resemblance whatsoever to the persons who were actually involved in the events described in this book.

ABOUT THE AUTHOR

Amie Streater is the associate pastor for financial stewardship at New Life Church. She is passionate about helping families recover from debt and overspending so they can walk in financial freedom and discover God's true calling for their lives. Amie came into full-time ministry in 2006 after fifteen years as an investigative newspaper reporter. She and her husband, Scott, live in Colorado Springs with their three little boys. Amie is an avid reader and writer and loves to travel. She also enjoys cooking and gardening, and with three boys, has become an expert at carpet cleaning and stain removal.